YOUR JOURNEY OF LIFE IS TO GET YOU
TO WAKE UP BUT IT'S NEVER EASY

YOUR JOURNEY OF LIFE

*Is to Get You to Wake Up but It's Never Easy:
My Journey to Awakened*

LIZABETH CACERES

Palmetto Publishing Group
Charleston, SC

Your Journey of Life Is to Get You to Wake Up but It's Never Easy
Copyright © 2019 by Lizabeth Caceres
All rights reserved

No portion of this book may be reproduced, stored in a retrieval system, or transmitted in any form by any means–electronic, mechanical, photocopy, recording, or other except for brief quotations in printed reviews, without prior permission of the author.

First Edition

Printed in the United States

ISBN-13: 978-1-64111-426-4
ISBN-10: 1-64111-426-6

In Loving Memory of my brother Robert Anthony Colon
January 18, 1973
November 22, 2016

INTRODUCTION

I sit up and look around. I see wooden bars in front of me. People who look like me are playing on the floor with their toys. I hear music, people singing—I don't know where its coming from, but it's loud. A lady with dark black hair, fragile and petite, approaches. I'm startled and scared. I don't know who she is. She hands me a juice cup and then puts her hands under my armpits and puts me on the floor. The room has large cages; I remember being pulled from the top. As I'm taken to the floor next to my twin sister, who looks just like me, the loud music and people speaking get louder and louder. I stand up on my two feet, too small to look through the glass in the room. I look over at the lady clapping her hands, waving them up, and saying, as I recall, "Amen!" But wait, where is Mama? Where is Papi?—as we say "Mom" and "Dad" in the Spanish language. Mama never allowed me to stop attending church until I left for college. What was it?

There was systematic chaos in my household that rocked the core fear in my being that has never been resolved or attended to: verbal abuse, emotional abuse by both parents, the suffering of my mother, sexual abuse by older men. Loud music, drugs, prostitution, suspicion of murder, death, deception within the family, witnessing sexual interactions of relatives with my father. This is the life I have known, though I longed to witness something different. I wanted out. I knew from a young child that I was different. I didn't know how different other than speaking the same language, I knew somewhere within I was different. I didn't belong, and because of this, I suffered hard, I suffered deep within my soul, I was broken down. The beautiful little girl within was broken into pieces and felt alone. Until the light shone, and shone brighter than the moment I was born into this human life.

CHAPTER 1
Safe Haven

This is where it all begins; the church family was my safe haven, so I thought at the time. My young life was full of turmoil, cries, pain, and misunderstandings, different from the lives of many around me on a daily basis. My appearance and characteristics were very different from others within my environment—my hair, the color of my skin, my tone, the way I spoke, how I talked. Many did not understand me. I could understand those around me at school, but I could also understand how my parents spoke to me in the home. Our language was different; I could only speak it in my home or with the people who looked relatively like me. I was timid, and why? What happened to me was not supposed to happen. I was a good girl; things like this do not happen to a little girl like me. This was the beginning of my known upbringing.

I hated weekends at home; the screaming and fighting between Mama and Papi were loud and scary. On many family road trips, Papi would someway, somehow end up drunk. Most often he would drive drunk, and in my early years I would lie in the back seat of the car and end up on the floor, hitting the back of the passenger seat where Mama was sitting. Papi would drive drunk, and on our journeys home I remember hearing both him and Mama screaming; he would often hit parked cars or hit the brakes to stop very hard. I often landed on the side of my head, hitting my left ear, and with extreme fear I would jump up and sit back on the seat and cry.

Many times, I would hear a loud thump or bang, as if the floors were shaking. I would run and hide in the closet until I could no longer hear anyone screaming. I wanted to be in a dark room with no noise. I felt safe in the dark room. I knew this was where I could speak with my angel. I would cry out and ask for the screaming to stop, to go away. I would slightly open the closet door and look out, listen, run to push the light switch on. *OK, it's clear. Should I go out and see what's going on?*

"OK," I would whisper to my sister, Leila.

She would say, "Lizabeth, don't go out, stay in the room."

As I opened the door, there was Papi. I could smell his breath; it smelled funny, like alcohol. The odor of his shirt smelled like gasoline. He certainly did not smell the same from earlier in the day. He did not speak the same, his eyes were red and scary, and as I watched him walk past my room to his room, he stumbled, gliding against the wall. I thought to myself, *Why is he that way?* I ran downstairs to see my mama crying; her face was red, hair sticking up, shirt bloody. I was frightened. I cried to see Mama like that, her nose bloody, her eyes red.

"Mama, why did Papi do that to you?"

"It's OK, go to your room."

I would then hear a knock on the door. It was a man in a dark uniform; the police would be called several times a month. Mama would say every time, "Everything is OK, Officer. My children's father came home drunk."

The officers would always ask the same question: "Are you OK, ma'am?"

"Yes, Officer," my mother would reply in her scared tone of voice.

This was a common ordeal to go through; I just never knew what would happen on the weekends. Papi was never around during the weekdays because of his work schedule. Friday and Saturday he would spend at Titi Isabel's husband's garage. His name was Kiko, and I considered him my uncle. Isabel was Papi's sister who lived here in the States: Papi had another sister, Rosi, in Puerto Rico. Isabel's husband, Kiko, rented a space where he worked on cars, fixing them up for friends and family to make a living. Papi would go there to help out; he mainly did all the paint jobs, while Kiko would do the major mechanical work.

I can remember one evening about ten or ten thirty at night. Mama was wondering where Papi was because we all had eaten dinner, and Papi was a no-show after work on a Friday night. Mama asked my sister and me to put on pajamas, and we gathered Carlos in his stroller and left the house.

I was extremely tired; it was a hot summer night. I asked Mama, "Where are we going?"

She said, "We are going to the garage to take some food to your dad."

I remember walking into the garage and not seeing Papi anywhere. Immediately I looked down and saw Papi with his pants down and Deborah with him. She ran away with no shirt on; I immediately ran off screaming and crying and hearing my mom scream at Papi. He was drunk and started yelling at Mama as if she were the one who had done something really bad. I just did not understand at the time why my aunt Deborah was there in the garage with my dad.

Over the years, the infidelity continued, not only with Deborah but also with another of Mama's sisters. Natalia, who was known as the "fast lady" around the small town I grew up in, also had sexual relations with Papi. I did not like the rumored gossip; I simply knew her as Mama's sister who deeply needed help. I could always see and feel the good in people. I never understood why an insult was used to identify certain members of the family. Natalia was so known by so many people. She was someone I knew, even as a child, wore a lot of makeup and was always superhyper with a can of beer in hand. The relationship she had with Mama was very toxic, as were her relationships with many others in the area. She would get into fights and was always in and out of prison. There were rumors around town from friends of Mama that Natalia had something to do with the murder of a prominent doctor. I wouldn't have been surprised if she knew something or was involved with the people who knew what actually happened. To this day, the murder of this prominent doctor is still a mystery.

Mama did not drive when I was a young child, and we walked everywhere until my sister and I were about thirteen years of age. Then Mama went and bought herself a blue small Chevy Nova. She got the courage and faith to trust and believe in herself that she could do things on her own. Even during the times when I thought things were getting better at home, I just knew it would not last long. Mama, as I remember, did the best she could. She always had a will and a determination to keep moving forward no matter what people said. She was such a hard worker. She always made us all breakfast before we headed off to school, even when she was so tired with dark circles under her eyes and breath that smelled like cigarette. She prepared a overnight bag for my older brother, Robert, when she knew he would take the school bus home to Grandma's after school, never really knowing the type of attitude Papi would have when he got home from work.

I longed for the stillness, the quietness, the laughter, the "good ole" happy times when Mama and Papi would hug and kiss. I always wanted to have some normalcy for as long as I can remember. At the age of four walking to preschool, I could sense that I did not belong. Still, my inner being, my inner knowing, was always to keep moving forward. Just to live daily, so that I could wake up tomorrow. I only felt safe in my home; as soon as I walked outside, I just knew that we as human beings were all different. That not everyone had the same thoughts or feelings or knowing that I did. I was timid; I was afraid to speak to others. The verbal abuse in my home is what kept me from moving forward in expressing myself as a child to want to learn and aspire to be. I was not shown to follow my dreams. There was no time for extracurricular activities, no time to run around with friends. What I witnessed were adults in a bedroom leaning over a dresser putting their faces over a powdery white substance that looked like baby powder. A lot of loud music and people, family, friends of family, and people unknown to me. "Go downstairs!" Papi would yell, and I would run to my room so fast, as if there were an evil, dark entity surrounding him. As if the dark entity were going to come after me and turn me into something or someone like him. I wondered, *Why is he acting this way? What did I do?* All I wanted was love from both Papi and Mama. Neither one of them had any time for me, Leila, Carlito, or Robert. At this age I never really understood why Robert was not with us as a family. He was my older brother; he should live with us. Robert was from Mama's previous marriage. He lived with Grandmom Justina on the weekends; she was Grandmom to me. I felt safe when Robert was with us; he protected us, his siblings. Late-night evenings that went by, and I cried myself to sleep and waited for the next morning to see Robert. It never made any sense for Robert to spend the night at Grandmom's house because four of her adult children and their children lived there. Mama's oldest sister who was rumored to have a daughter by the pastor of the church. Honestly no one knew for sure, and no one would ever know. Robert and this daughter always seemed to be together, playing sports.

Papi's brother Eugene from Puerto Rico came to live with us for some time. The talk in the family was that the week he came from Puerto Rico, he got involved in a relationship with a woman, and she became pregnant with his child, a little girl just a few years younger than Leila and me. She was a lady that Mama did not speak highly of. She was a single mom already to a little girl. She was also known to do drugs and someone who partied and would leave her kids with different babysitters. Tio Eugene had many different ladies in his life. I never saw him living in his own home' he slept in one of the empty rooms in my house. He always had a bottle of alcohol, a well-known brand from Puerto Rico called Bacardi. Tio would get locked out sometimes and call Mama to open the door; he would be so drunk he could barely walk up the stairs. I loved Tio Eugene because I knew he was from the land that my grandparents were from; to me that was special enough at the time. He did not speak very much of the English language. But something horrible happened that changed my mind one summer evening of 1983. Tio Eugene came home; I could hear him downstairs as I played with my Barbie dolls. I heard a loud thump and ran down the stairs to see Tio Eugene on the floor in the hallway with blood all over his arm. There was blood all through the hallway and on the bedroom floor. It was scary; I thought Tio was dead. When Mama turned him over, he had a needle sticking out, like a needle I had seen at the doctor's office. I knew it was not good because Mama would scream and yell at Papi. The ambulance would come and check Tio out, and he would continue to drink and do the same thing again and again. For some time Tio would clean up his act and live with a girlfriend, a much younger girl that he got pregnant and had two little girls with. But the relationship did not last long because the drugs got the best of him. The same thing happened to him again, with the needle and passing out. Papi said he had to go back to Puerto Rico, because so many people were dying. The alcohol and the partying never stopped in my home. This went on for a couple of years.

CHAPTER 2

What Did It All Mean for Me?

September of 1985 I was eight years old. The night, which I thought was a celebration, turned out to be the worst experience of my life. Papi came home telling Mama to ready, get the kids ready, because "we're all going to my friend's house in Coatesville." My thoughts were that while it seemed very far as a child, it was only about twenty-five minutes from the little apartment I grew up in. The night seemed long; Papi was drinking with the old man of the house. He had two nice daughters, Lisa and Jackie; I remember one being very skinny with long black hair; the other had a pale skin tone with light-brown, yellowish curly hair. She looked like a Barbie doll; she was beautiful and looked like her mother. Jackie was a very protective individual but had a knack for boys.

The night grew later and later; I sat on the couch, leaning against my twin sister. Music was still playing loudly; Papi came over asking if we wanted to lie down. Mama carried me into the room where all of the coats were. I lay down in a dark room, musty smelling and cluttered; as I looked up, I could see a TV on. Without paying close attention, I fell asleep. I couldn't keep my eyes open; they felt heavy. I felt scared and cold. I could hear the music still playing and people talking loudly. A big boy came over to the bed; he put his hands under my dress. His fingers went into my panties. I did not know what to do. He said, "Shhhhh…" I started to cry because I was scared; the tears just rolled down my face and kept rolling down. I could feel the warmth of my tears. I wanted to scream, but I couldn't. I felt as though I couldn't breathe. The boy then put something in my mouth; I didn't know what it was, I couldn't see, the room was dark. "It" felt warm. I could hear him say, "Do you like my penis in your mouth?" While I lay on the bed, he then said not to move or say anything.

As I lay on the bed crying, my mom entered the room to check on me. She said, "What's the matter?" At this point the boy had run out of the room. "Do you want to go home?" Mama asked. I nodded my head yes. She grabbed all of our coats from that room and left. It was the beginning of the worst day of my life. Mama and Papi had to work; Mama had Jackie take care of us girls and little Carlos. Jackie was great, and I wanted to tell her what her brother did to me, but I was scared to tell anyone. I was angry at my dad for many years. I started to hate him, to blame him and Mama for what I had gone through. I hated to be around people at gatherings. I wanted to be alone. I felt safe alone.

The drinking did not stop. Papi would come home drunk at night, and Mama would yell and scream at him. "Do you know what time it is? Where were you?" Mama would be in Papi's face and follow him to the room, screaming and yelling. I would peek through the doorway and watch. When I did look out, I could see Papi entering the bathroom while Mama said, "No, not in my bathroom." She grabbed him by the arm, and he pushed her away and hit her in the head as she fell to the ground. I ran out of the bedroom and screamed so loudly, loud enough to wake up my siblings. Mama had blood all over her head and face. She didn't look like she was breathing. I touched her face; she was warm. I ran to call for help. I knocked on the next-door neighbor's house, and the lady called the ambulance and the police. Papi stayed behind to care for us, but Mama didn't come home for a couple of weeks. The officers did not say anything to Papi, but I remember after several days he had to brush our hair, dress us, and send us off to school. Then he would drive us to see Mama in the hospital. He did what he could do at the time. I never did see Grandmom or Mama's sisters come around to help or to see Mama. I knew she was alone; I knew she felt like no one was with her. But I was assured that God was with her. That she was a strong person. Many people I thought were her friends did not come around. My heart ached for Mama; the house was disorganized without her. The drinking had to stop; I thought it was done, but things began to get worse.

About five years went by; the age of thirteen was better for me. I was more knowledgeable of my surroundings and still never really had a close relationship with Papi. I always wondered why he never showed affection for Mama. I also felt no one really cared about what happened to me. What if I told Mama? Would she believe me? If I told my older brother, what would he say to me? I put my thoughts together: *He is my older brother; he should believe me. Who wouldn't? But what happened to me should not have ever happened to me. Whom do I trust at this point?*

Since what happened to me in my eyes was allowed, it affected my self-esteem, my belief in God, my belief in angels, my belief in miracles, and my belief in faith. Growing up in my household was hard for me. I contemplated dying and being with Jesus and all the people surrounding him. Who would see that I'd hurt myself, who would see that I'd died and gone to heaven? Who would pay attention, who would care? No one cared what had been done to me. Not even God. I was not protected; I was not cared for the way a child should be, and protected. As I continued to mature, grow, and attend school, I held onto what happened to me within myself, never telling anyone.

Deuteronomy 31:6: "Be strong and courageous. Do not be afraid or terrified because of them, for the Lord your God goes with you; he will never leave you nor forsake you."

I never let go of my past transgression, my adolescent years as well as my young-adult memories are all inconsistent with my true self. While I had an affinity for God, I found myself in my early teens falling in and out of sin. I found it hard to stay out of sin. Was it because of what happened to me? I never let go of what happened to me. At thirteen to fourteen years of age, I became more aware of my body, feeling and seeing changes. I started to have feelings for boys; I felt a strong attraction. I prayed to God and asked him to remove the past thoughts that haunted me for years. As with everything one experiences in life, it was a test from God. I was afraid to question God. Who was I to do so? I was supposed to live each day and be happy that I got a chance to wake up. But my belief and trust in others was forever tainted. I learned to live with my guard up.

On June 22, 1991, I was fourteen years old. Mama, Papi, Leila, and my brother Carlos celebrated that summer by going to Dorney Park, an amusement park. Going to the amusement park every summer when school let out was a great time, something to look forward to with family. This was a day to see all the people Papi worked with. Many of his coworkers were friends who visited Papi at the house. Mama would cook meals for many.

There was one particular young individual, a recent high-school graduate, who worked with Papi. His name was Miguel. His older brother Alex worked with Papi for well over ten years. Miguel always told Papi how beautiful his daughters were. I always chuckled inside. My attention was drawn to Miguel; he was cute, and he watched me at the park. Leila and I walked around the amusement park and got on rides together. We ran into Miguel and his friend, who asked if we could all get on rides together. I did not hesitate; I said, "Yes, sure," with a smile on my face. Miguel had a smile on his face as well, but one thing I got to notice was that he had a dry sense of humor. I was only fourteen at the time, and he was eighteen so I thought it was just cool to hang out with him. He kept saying he'd never dated a Spanish girl.

I said, "Wow, you're Spanish; how can that be?" He said he'd always been attracted to white girls. I told him, "I can be the first to change that"; he flirtatiously laughed. The chemistry was there; we hung out together the rest of the day at Dorney Park. We held hands, even sat together to eat and talk. He talked about how cool my dad was, and that he was a hard worker. I could hear the nervousness in his tone when he said he was afraid of Papi. He had seen him get angry at work with other coworkers. I was in the eighth grade. He was a high school graduate, so the thought of him already completing school was awesome to me; it was cool in my young, naïve eyes.

When the weekends came around, Miguel would call me and ask me how I was doing in school. I started to enjoy the attention he gave me. Papi really didn't like the fact that Miguel would call me; he would always say, "Focus on school, not someone I work with! Yes, he's a hard worker but not someone to have a future with." The weekend phone calls began to be daily. Then Miguel asked my father if he could pick me up to go see a movie. My father did not allow it, but he said Miguel could come to the house to see me. That was exciting to me. We made plans for a Saturday; my mom cooked dinner, but Miguel was a no-show. His excuse was that his car broke down. Luckily I had a friend, Tracy, who lived down the road from him. She mentioned he was driving around the Oxford area with some other Spanish girl. I was distraught that Miguel had lied to me, but I also did not understand his intentions, or his intentions at that moment. What was he thinking? He called me several days later to express how sorry he was and that he would make it up to me. I believed him and thought it was nice that he'd called me.

The days went by, the weeks went by, the months went by, until I received a phone call that Miguel was in town and wanted to come by my house to see me. I told him to come over, and he showed up with a friend. I knew it was him because I could hear loud music from two blocks away. My heart started pounding; I ran outside to double check, and sure enough it was him. He was with his friend William. As soon as Miguel got out of the car, he came right over gave me a hug. He then bent down to kiss me, which was awkward and not something I was really looking forward to. I did get a strange feeling of *I should not be doing this*; it did not feel right. But then, my thoughts were *Whatever, it was just a kiss*. I then began to think, *OK, this guy who is older than me really likes me; it's awesome to have someone like me*. I befriended his family, or so I thought. I would call his home, and his mother would answer the phone in a sweet, loving manner. She would relate messages, and at times he would call me but many times ignore my calls.

I continued to go to church every Sunday to pray for Miguel and his family. One late Friday evening, he came over; we sat outside, and he confided in me that his older brother used to date a lady who lived not too far from me. He said he could not stand the sight of this lady, that she was the reason his brother had gotten addicted to drugs and later committed suicide. Her name was Sandra, and she had three daughters, one of whom I had attended elementary school with. I lived across the street from where she lived, which was an apartment complex that was owned and operated by the state and local county for lower-income families. Her youngest daughter was his deceased brother's daughter. This woman did not have a good reputation as far as I can remember. Sandra had gotten married at the age of fifteen, had a baby, dropped out of high school, and was known to have sexual relations with several men. Also, at that time she was known to be dating a young guy,

Angelo who was not from the area. The talk around town was that this younger guy she was dating was from Delaware. Growing up I never cared to understand, but that relationship was different; I would see them around town, and the guy would act like he was Miguel's nieces father. Sandra's boyfriend would stare as he would drive by Mama's house all the time. Sandra would drive by and always give the evil eye. It was not my fault their relationship was sour. Angelo was known to be very promiscuous and flirtatious. I thought he had it in for my titi, Nancy, Mama's younger sister who also grew up with Sandra and knew her very well. Nancy would say, "Look at him," as he would drive by in his car playing loud music. He would drive slow and just watch us. It would get on my aunt's nerves, and she would be annoyed, knowing he had a girlfriend; there was no need to look at other women.

I really felt sad for Miguel to experience a brother that he looked up to committing suicide at a very young age. Miguel would come over frequently, and we'd hang out and talk about life in general, but things never went as far as serious relationship. I was only fourteen at the time; I looked at him like a big brother. The feelings were not the same anymore. I wanted more, more maturity, more desires. I also heard from his sister-in-law that Miguel was a player; he had a girlfriend in another state that he was sexually involved with. When I confronted Miguel about it, he did not deny it. Apparently it was someone who was much older with kids. So my thoughts and depressive thinking crept up, and all I could think of was how and why boys only wanted to simply hurt girls.

During this time in my life, the issues in my family life were quite complicated. I used to babysit my little cousin, Natalia son's Brian, who was born out of wedlock. Because Natalia was on drugs and working the streets, baby Brian would often be left with family members and not really cared for. It was known that one of Mama's sisters was only listed as a guardian just to get a check from the state for watching over him. Mama's younger sister cashed in on thousands of dollars, but there was nothing to show for it; Brian didn't have clothes that fit him and was always left with other family members. Brian also had a little half sister who was a year younger than him; her father was another man. Both kids were in the foster care system with the potential of being adopted by unknown people. I loved this little boy as if he were my little brother; Mama was able to bring him home and sign all paperwork with the county and state within a year of him living in our home. Once the caseworker said my aunt Natalia had lost all parental privileges, we were able to adopt Brian as our own. Having him become a part of my immediate family was a humbling experience. We changed his last name, and from that moment on I had another brother, now three in total, which made up five children Mama and Papi were parents to.

Along with the adoption came gossip from Mama's family. Along came Brian's biological mother, Natalia, to interfere. She would come with one of Papi's friends she was living with to our home frequently on weekends to drink and party. Whenever Brian misbehaved and Mama disciplined him in some way or another, Natalia would always interfere. An argument of some sort would entail; witnessing the exchanges between Natalia and Mama was never easy for me internally. I always felt like Natalia was very ungrateful; her children were all taken from her due to her own inner demons of drugs, alcohol, and prostitution. I learned about the prostitution from a man I overheard speaking aloud to Mama about her own sister. I did not understand what the meaning was at that time; I just knew it was being with different and many men to feed her drug habit. Mama did the best she could a loving, caring mother who worked very hard to get where she was at the time. One thing for sure: it was never enough for Mama's seven sisters. There was always something to complain or gossip about within the family.

CHAPTER 3

Hatred and Confusion

At this point in my life I was beginning to hate boys. They all reminded me of what had happened at the age of eight. I decided I would never speak to Miguel again. Months passed, and about a year later, my parents were preparing a quinceañera (a Sweet Fifteen birthday bash) for my sister and me. It's a time of celebration and entering womanhood. Leila and I were super excited; we only wanted to invite special people we'd grown up with plus all of our family and our parents' friends. This quinceañera was going to be spectacular. There were many people trying to be our friends just to get invited.

Papi worked so hard during this time; we took many trips to Philadelphia, a forty-five-minute drive to the city to buy decorations and centerpieces and do dress fittings. Many of my school friends did not understand the significance of my party. Most were "gringos," as we called the Caucasians. Mama got the church scheduled and asked many people within the community to cook for the party. Papi scheduled a reputable salsa band from Delaware. Mama got one of her friends to make our dresses and our birthday cake. She spent a whole year sewing up all the girls' dresses; my sister and I had fourteen girls and boys in our Sweet Fifteen court. We even had a junior miniboy and -girl to carry our crowns, which were put on at the church ceremony as we were blessed and prayed for about our entrance into womanhood. Having our parents put a high heel on us in front of hundreds of people was a surreal experience.

A quinceañera is very much like a wedding. Leila and I created an invite list of our school friends, parents' friends, community members, and lots of family members from all over the East Coast, north and south, all the way to Puerto Rico and Florida. Just about five hundred were on the list for invites. My family was well-known in the Puerto Rican community. I can't say we were the richest family, but we were hardworking middle class.

As the day got closer, the excitement built up and chaos started. So, on April 20, 1992, at about eight in the morning, Mama woke Leila and me. I woke up excited and looking forward to being a princess for the day. All I wanted to do was put on my dress and get my makeup done. My hair was already done; we had gotten our hair done the night prior in a small salon, one of the best in Coatesville, Pennsylvania, called Dukes. The morning started out as a day of pampering, makeup, and nails, which we were not accustomed to. Once the large puffy white dress was put on, I felt like a princess who was going to the ball. There were about twenty cars parked outside in front of my house—so many types of Toyota lowriders playing loud salsa music, car horns blowing in celebrations of our Sweet Sixteen. It was such an awesome feeling that so many people in my neighborhood, so many family and friends, showed so much love.

As I got ready to get in one of the limos, I felt like a princess; it was so hard getting into the car but also bittersweet, and I watched Leila get in another car. We drove around town honking horns in celebration before heading to the church. As we drove around, we saw many of our friends and family come out and wave their hands in celebration. I glanced and saw Angelo as he stared looking out of a window in a nearby apartment complex.

Once we got to the church our party group (court) made two lines in front of the entrance. It was beautiful; the pastor of the church came outside to greet the both of us and our court. The ceremony was miraculous; thanking God for our birth to this point in our lives was a humbling experience. All the hurt, the sorrow…I could release and let it go. This meant a new beginning; a new life began from here. I had the power to learn from the early beginnings,

Once we got to the hall where we would have the birthday celebration, we were all welcomed at the community center hall as we walked in all of our family members, our friends already gathered together as we entered. My older brother, Robert, and his girlfriend at the time, Kristen, were the first two faces I saw; he looked happy for his twin sisters. As I entered I was overwhelmed by the abundance of cheers and music playing with singers on the platform stage. My sister and I gathered around our court for a remarkable show. We danced as the musicians sang; then we invited all to join in. It was an awesome experience.

Shortly after the dance, our parents sat us each on a princess chair made out of wicker to remove our flat shoes and put on our first high-heeled shoe. I remember feeling like Cinderella. There were so many people from all over Pennsylvania, New York, Delaware, and New Jersey. The news spread like wildfire; it was a night where I met some interesting boys from Delaware. Again I saw Angelo drive by my birthday venue, and my heart pounded. But I knew he was older than I was, so my focus was on someone who was at my party and the same age as myself. I did meet a boy from Delaware; his name was Joshua, and he came to my party with relatives of his, who worked with my father. Joshua was fifteen years old; I thought he was so cool and could really dance salsa like a professional dancer. His moves reminded me of my older brother, Robert. There were so many people laughing, dancing, eating having a good ole time. The singing of "Happy Birthday" was amazing; it felt really good to be center of attention. Leila and I cut the beautiful four-tier cake, and we smashed each other with cake and had a lot of fun with it. We also went to each of the tables to hand out cake to all who attended. I couldn't have asked for a better Sweet Fifteen birthday bash. The party was a success.

CHAPTER 4

Cancer, Death, Changes Within

The rest of the year was amazing. Until I got news that my mom's younger sister, my titi Nancy, was diagnosed with ovarian cancer. It was devastating news for the whole family, especially my mom. Nancy and her three boys spent a lot of time with my family. By the time she was sixteen years old, she had her first baby; by age twenty-two she already had three healthy babies. I remember when she had her third baby boy; he was almost born in my kitchen. I remember her going into labor and Mama calling the ambulance.

Nancy didn't like going to the doctors; shortly after giving birth she was supposed to go back to see her doctors, but she didn't. I know she experienced a lot of pain and constant had trouble using the bathroom. She carried a box of Ex-lax chocolate that was supposed to help her go to the bathroom. I honestly don't know if it did any good. There were a lot of hospital visits, testing, blood draws, and medications. Nancy lost a lot of weight up until surgery to remove a cyst on her ovary; something unexpected happened during surgery and her whole colon needed to be removed because the cancer had spread. Removing the whole colon meant that she needed to live with a colostomy bag for the rest of her life. It was inserted into her abdomen, and she was treated with chemotherapy and radiation.

Nancy was a trouper during that time. I always knew she would die and be with Grandmom, who had died three years before Nancy got really sick. Nancy fought so hard for her children; she loved her boys. She was dedicated, always looking for love as well. She was beautiful, and she taught me so much. She was so ladylike and so particular. When Nancy was twenty-four years old, the news in the family was that she was in remission. At the time that meant she was cured and would get better. I remember having vivid nightmares of myself in a coffin as if I were seeing my own funeral. That happened over the years. I did not want anything to happen to Nancy because she was my favorite aunt in the whole world. She was the one I could confide in and share my feelings with, and she helped me with homework. I could talk to her about boys, school, and my parents. Leila

Nancy lived three blocks from my house, so after school my sister Leila and I would walk to her apartment complex. The walk was not long so Mama and Papi would not mind. We had a curfew; Mama worked long hours, so after school Leila, Carlos, and I would work on homework and call our friends over the phone. We always made plans to hang out at my titi Nancy's apartment complex. Papi never really minded. He would go to work in the morning, come home the same time we got off the school bus, and go right to sleep. He never paid any attention to any of us, unless it was the weekend and he was drunk. Nancy's apartment complex was the hangout, and Papi wouldn't know who would be at the apartment. He only knew that the three of us were all together. Nancy was the strongest person I knew at the time. There were times when I felt abandoned by her actions because I helped with babysitting her boys. Mama had seven sisters, all with different personalities, and two cousins very close in age with myself and Leila.

Robert was involved in sports, so he spent a lot of time after school with his friends. If he wasn't playing football he was skateboarding all over town with his friends. He was older, so she hung out with the cool guys. Everyone lived at Grandmom's house, so that's where we would always find Robert. His friends all lived on the same block, so he would beg Mama to stay at Grandmom's because he would go fishing and hunting and play football. He was so active all the time, and Grandpa and Grandmom always supported him. He was the first grandson, so he was adored by everyone. Mama had seven sisters and four brothers. As a teenager I remember at one point about six adult aunts and uncles all lived with Grandmom and Grandpa, and I never really understood why until I got older.

There were many changes going on within myself and in the people around me. Grandmom's health was deteriorating while Nancy was in remission. I would go to school as usual, come home, and stay in my room listening to music, singing, and drawing or reading books. Anything I could get my hands on, I would read. We didn't have much so even if the books were adult novels given to me for free, I read them. I was always intrigued by spiritual books, the messages of God, prophets, and angels. When I did not read, I sat in stillness and prayed. Talking to God, I always felt as if someone was with me, outside of me, who would always listen to my asking, someone who always put a smile on my face. It was similar to an out-of-body experience, as if I could just reach out my hand and feel a presence. This spirit, this entity, this angel guide, was with me through all of my experiences, my classes, my exams, when I walked alone, when I sat in stillness alone in my bedroom. This person was with me. I didn't have many friends, so I depended on God.

While I enjoyed going to a Pentecostal church along with my Grandmom and Grandpa and most times with my aunts, I never really had an attached relationship with Grandmom. I only knew her as Mama's mother and nothing else. She was someone I was afraid of; as a young child, I only knew her as someone who always screamed at everyone, especially Mama. I remember her good-smelling food; I can only remember her yellow Puerto Rican rice with beans and some corn she would throw in the pot. I honestly can't remember any other type of food she cooked because her priorities where her other children and their children. My cousins were her priorities; I can't particularly say that she cared for me, or Leila or Carlos. I think it's because the relationship she had with Mama was tainted, although I never really understood why; I just had the memories Mama told Leila and myself. Now that I look back, I never saw Papi hold a conversation with Grandmom. The only good memory I held in my thoughts was a Sunday evening service; we walked to Grandmom's, and as we got ready for church Grandmom brushed my hair into a ponytail and braided my hair. That's a memory I hold dear, because it was the only time I ever got that close to her. I remember what she smelled like, a musty floral smell with a hint of lemon.

Mama was at work when she called home. I ran to the phone and answered. She told me that Grandmom was sick and transported to the hospital.

My response to Mama was "Is she dead?" In an instant I could see her body lying in a casket.

Mama said, "No, she is alive in the hospital; she had a stroke." I did not know what a stroke meant at that time, but I knew it was bad. I remember the commotion, the screaming of my aunts and uncles at Natalia. She would come and go, only come around to shower and go out onto the streets to sleep with men for money to get drugs to soothe her fix. Grandmom would scream and yell at her, but there was no talking to get through to Natalia. She had no respect for herself or others; she had a child by a married man, disrupting his marriage, and more children by different men. She would leave her babies with Grandmom and disappear for days on end without anyone knowing where she was. This particular day, she showed up on a day Grandmom was not feeling well and was being very disrespectful toward Grandmom, as everyone put it, and Grandmom became very ill; her blood pressure went up dangerously high to the point the ambulance was called, and after that point she would not come back to her home. All of this happened a few weeks before Christmas; Grandmom died on Mama's birthday. I did not know what to think of her death. I did not cry, nor did I have any emotions because I knew her soul was no longer with her body. I remember feeling her hands, her body very hard and cold, lifeless, in her casket. I could see everyone at her funeral crying and being very dramatic. I could hear her voice in my thoughts and a warmth of love and affection. I could see her standing next to her body and looking at everyone who walked past. She seemed sad. I was confused because in life she was not that way with me. I had always felt she only had love, an affection, a motherly relationship with her other grandchildren, but not with her own daughter Lydia's kids, me being one of them. But now she was different, so loving; a yellowish white light surrounding her body was amazing.

    The evening of Grandmom's funeral, everyone went back to her home to gather and talk about her. As I sat on the couch listening to Mama's sisters talk about Grandmom's belongings, I could hear three of Mama's sisters argue about who was keeping dresses and costume jewelry that were Grandmom's. The argument got louder, and I went to Mama to let her know what was going on. Mama went upstairs to address the situation, and my mom's oldest sister yelled and looked directly into my eyes, calling me a "big-mouth" for telling my mom that they were all fighting over who was keeping what of Grandmom's. In my young mind, I found it disrespectful to go through all of her stuff when it had only been a few hours after she was laid to rest.

The tension in the family became so bad the energy in the home, and people around me became overwhelming that at one point I did not want to live in this life anymore. I contemplated ending my life. One morning after my mother was yelling at Leila and me to clean the house, I took a whole bottle of Tylenol. I wanted to die in my own bed in peace. That evening, I was required to go with Mama and Papi to her brother's house for a birthday party. I felt weak; after drinking some soda, I felt dizzy and passed out. I woke up in the hospital, going in and out of consciousness while the nurse pumped me with some sort of charcoal substance. Eventually into a hospital in the Philadelphia area for about thirty days. This is where I felt a connection to others around me, and I learned how to sit in silence and pray and meditate. I learned how to control my anger, and let go of what was internally bothering me. I learned that anger or being upset was only temporary, I learned that I was not the only one who had family problems. I learned that life is full of challenges, I learned that talking to others helps me let go of what "bothers" me.

We all have stories of some sort, that may help someone in "their" journey. It is what we do with the negative experiences is what determines our outcomes in life. You can either choose the left continue the road to negative situations or you can choose the right way for an extraordinary outcome of liberation of the "mind." I left the institution, stronger than entering with a different way of looking at things that came at me. While I thought that everything was easy, it was a continual battle to survive this humanistic life.

CHAPTER 5

Adjusting, Lust, Questioning Life

I remember praying for a larger home, where I could have my own bedroom since I always shared a room with Leila. Mama and Papi were so excited that finally we were going to be buying a home of our own. A four-bedroom home—wow, that was exciting!

Leila and Carlos, along with myself, had gone searching for a home with our parents. We saw about three houses, which were fairly small. Then one Friday afternoon we looked at a large home that had everything Mama wanted: the large kitchen, a yard for all of us to play in, space for Papi to plant his vegetables, a garden he'd always wanted, and of course space to work on cars. We even had a two-car garage that also had space to fit up to four-plus cars.

Within a three-month span, we were all moved into the house. I did not get my own bedroom, which I had initially wanted and prayed for; I still had to share a room with Leila. My room was very small; Leila and I shared a daybed similar to a twin-size bed, and underneath was a pull-out mattress the same size. We also shared a dresser with six drawers. Initially I thought it would be just Leila and me, but Mama said her sister Deborah would be living with us until she got a place of her own. Deborah recently had gotten out of prison for stealing checks from Grandpa; she got five years. I had mixed emotions and did not trust her; she was the one I remembered clearly with my own eyes with Papi. I could not forgive this woman, but because she was Mama's sister, who was I to say anything or talk back to Mama?

However, it became horrific when Mama said, "Well, she will be sleeping in your room with Leila."

That was when my whole world shook; I was immediately devastated. I asked Mama where Deborah would sleep. "I have a small twin-size bed."

"She will sleep with you," Mama replied.

I was a tiny 98 pounds and had to share my bed with someone who was over 150 pounds or more. I never understood what Mama was thinking to have done this to me. I felt betrayed by both parents. The stay lasted for almost two and a half years. The stay turned into gossip about me and my immediate family: it turned into the extended family talking about me being a spoiled brat, it turned into the family talking to me without respect, and it caused the relationship between myself and my mother to become estranged. There were many smacks in my face by Mama, because of her own siblings.

Carlos, Brian, and Robert shared the master bedroom with bunkbeds. We also had the attic turned into a bedroom for Mama's cousin whom she had helped raise since the age of eleven. He was and is like an older brother, quiet, smart, and articulate, a good person. He always kept to himself and always was willing to help family. Ivan is his name; while he initially lived with Grandmom and Grandpa, there were so many people living in that house that he didn't have any privacy of his own, and from what Mama had said in the past, he was mistreated in that house, so she took him in to raise. Mama watched over him until he graduated from high school, and Papi helped buy him a car; and off to college he went.

Ivan turned the attic into a master suite, furnished with a separate living-room space and fish tank, so serene and so calm. I always knew when he was home; we all had to be quiet and respectful. I always felt protected when Ivan was home, because you never knew how Papi's demeanor would be if he got drunk on any given day or weekend. If I ever felt scared or if I noticed an argument was going to start between Papi and Mama, I would run to Ivan for safety.

Moving into the new house I thought was the greatest thing that had ever happened. I started high school; I was proud because I knew that in three years I would be graduating high school and off to college just like Ivan. I had dreams and aspirations to get out, have a career, and raise a family differently from how I was raised. I had many distractions along the way. The new house was across the street from a private Catholic high school. I used to walk to and from high school, so when school let out I would always run into a girl who looked just like me: Puerto Rican with long black hair. Jessica was her name. We instantly became really good friends, and I came to find out she was a cousin of my cousin. Small world. Her aunt had a daughter with my uncle Eugene. I always knew of the two daughters my uncle had, but I never had a close relationship with his oldest daughter. All I knew was that she was close in age to Carlos . I always knew the women my uncle dealt with were simply into drugs or accepted that lifestyle.

A lot of planning took place when we moved into the house. The kitchen needed to be knocked down and redone. All the rooms needed to be painted, but Mama said in due time it would all take place. The kitchen was not a rush, as Papi would always say. The outside was amazingly beautiful, but the interior was in need of a lot of work and updating. Papi was really only worried about working in the garage and working in the garden—but also entertaining his friends on the weekends. The house became the go-to place to hang out on the weekends. There were lots of parties, gatherings where the extended family would socialize and take part in their extracurricular activities such as strong alcohol, cocaine, and marijuana use. No one ever really paid attention to my internal or external needs. I was bullied in school this same time; two Caucasian girls in a grade ahead of me, both bigger than myself, shared the same study hall. They walked by me chewing gum, only to spit it into my hair. I did nothing for fear of retaliation. I felt like I was a walking, ticking time bomb.

So the loud noise became a social norm in my early teenage years. Every holiday, every birthday party was celebrated in the house. However, while there was always family around one could feel the love in the air. The warmth was so heavy in the house at all times. It was sometimes very overwhelming; my mind, my thoughts always cried to God for a change. The energy in the house was always too much to bear. I strived to be alone, to cry, to vent, to scream out why I had the life I had at this very moment. Mama always worked nights; she was home while we were at school and when it was time for us to go to bed. Papi worked very hard; as far as I can remember, he was always working. One thing for sure is that when I needed something for school or clothes, Papi was there to provide. But I can't really remember ever feeling love and compassion from Papi.

Jazmin, Natalia's daughter, became pregnant, and she did not have a place to stay or live, so Mama moved her into the house. Natalia never really raised any of her children; all were taken from her by the state. One thing I need to make clear is that Mama had seven sisters and four brothers; you would think that from the kindness of any of their hearts they would have helped their own sister out. None were in the position to help but rather lie to the state and act as if they were financially there for the children. Mama was the only one who had a home, and they all knew Mama's door was always open to family. Jazmin, being a teenage mom at the time, needed the help and guidance and some sort of normalcy of a family. Leila and I embraced her with love and compassion and with help in any way we could. Jazmin grew up like our third sister; we loved her and continue to love her and her children.

The house became extremely cluttered; only having one full bathroom and four bedrooms with so many people in the house became disastrous. We made the best of it; by the time Jazmin came home with her baby boy, Deborah was out of the house and moved two blocks away to a one-bedroom apartment. Shortly after, she moved in with a man she met from a halfway house who was soon to be released from the prison system.

As I was approaching sixteen years of age, Jessica and I were like two peas in a pod. She had a close connection with my cousin, and I had a connection with someone my family did not approve of. I didn't understood why at the time; he was not Puerto Rican, and he was twenty-two years old with a car and always drove around town with older girls who did not have careers, basically a group of alcoholics. I thought this guy was cool; he was not from the area, which drew my attention. One time he drove by my parents' house and stopped while Jessica and I were hanging out. As we were sitting in a group, we exchanged phone numbers. He used to call me, but we never had a serious conversation. The phone calls were almost always about how beautiful I was and how we should be in a serious relationship. I couldn't do that because I had aspirations beyond high school. I always mentioned to him that my main focus at the time was to graduate from high school and then go on to college outside of Pennsylvania. I wanted to become a business professional and start my own business. That friendship/relationship shortly dwindled because of his lifestyle. I knew I needed more out of life and respected my father's decisions and input in life. "I want a man like my dad" is something I used to say in my head, a hardworking man but without the cheating aspects, someone who took care of his children financially.

The first year of living in the house was amazing, a lot of laughs, a lot of love, and a lot of painting and revamping the house to a more modern look. On the downside it also came with a lot of torment and cries. The drinking and weekend gatherings got out of control on some nights. The house was the hub of all the alcohol and food; friends of Papi and Mama would all hang out and eat and drink beers at the house. The music was loud.

It was getting super late one particular evening. More and more people showed up, all friends of Papi's; they all gathered in the basement of the house. Leila and I were not allowed to go downstairs; I sat in the living room and talked to Nancy as she lay on the couch. As I sat on the couch, I could smell marijuana seeping from downstairs up into the living room, and I just wondered in my thoughts about how this was the not life I wanted to live. GOD, *please help me become a better person or be a part of a family that is different than what I know at this moment.* The evening went on, and it got later; Papi was so drunk, his eyes were bloodshot red, and he seemed to stumble up and down the stairs. Mama was getting tired and was asking him to lower the music and start to clean up. As the music went down, the voices seem to be lowered too, as I couldn't hear anyone from upstairs. Mama was starting to get agitated and yelled downstairs through the basement door. Papi came running up the stairs screaming that it was his house and he would say when everyone was to leave. As I looked back into the kitchen, it seemed as though Papi was going to put his hands on Mama. As I saw him raise his hands, I ran to dial 911; as an operator came on the line, Papi saw me on the phone, ran downstairs, and got the machete. He came right back upstairs and yelled, "You better hang up the phone right now!" I screamed and looked at Nancy; I seemed to see not her but a shadowy white light surrounding her body, as she could not move.

Papi said, "Now that you called 911, you are going to pay." He grabbed me by the neck.

I looked into his eyes and cried out, "Papi, please stop! You don't know what you're doing."

As he raised the machete and was in the moment of cutting my head off, a bright light came through the front door, which had been knocked down. It was a police officer holding a gun; he said, "Drop it, Juan." Papi ran off downstairs at the precise moment the police officer ran after Papi and sprayed him with pepper spray. All I could do was scream with horror at my father. At the same time, I knew it was divine intervention from the angels who surrounded me and no one but God who intervened at that precise moment.

Papi was taken into custody and spent five long days in prison, and after that we as a family went to family counseling. Later, it was mentioned in counseling that Papi had a problem with prescription medication and mixing it with alcohol, which led to him not remembering what he did the previous night.

Nancy's health started to deteriorate; she became sicker than ever before. Her cancer came back, and this time it had spread to other organs in her body. She needed to get back to chemotherapy and radiation to kill what was invading her body. Mama or I would go pick her up every day so she wouldn't be alone in her apartment. This was a trying time for the family; watching her lie in pain on the couch was not easy. Her three boys spent a lot of time running around the house; Mama fed them and took care of them, and I did as well. Nancy was a trouper, always positive, and always praying to God for a miracle. Her favorite psalm of the Bible was Psalm 40:1–17: "I waited patiently for the Lord; he turned to me and heard my cry." She read that every day, and every day she read through the Bible. When she was in pain, which was most of the time, I could see her reading the Bible. Nancy never gave up; she wore a bandana to cover her head as her hair was falling out. She never wanted anyone to feel sorry for her but to be happy in the present moment. She loved her boys, and they were what drove her to keep fighting for her life. Up until her last breath, I remember her saying to please not put plastic sneakers on her boys. She loved them with all her might, and I know she has been with her boys into adulthood.

The last year was a hard year for me, as I was in the eleventh grade. I was confused about life and death, questioning God. I knew Nancy was going to pass to the other side because a week prior to her death I had a dream of seeing myself in the casket. It was a sign from source, God, the angels, that one close to me was going to be entering the other side. I remember those exact words but never really understood that it would happen so quickly, or perhaps I did not want to acknowledge that in the near future Nancy would be leaving the family and not be here in the physical.

Her funeral was so beautiful. Titi Nancy looked peacefully asleep, and I knew she was no longer suffering in pain but that she could see us all from the other side. This was the third death in the family: Grandmom, one of mamas younger brother and now Nancy. This was all too much for me and too familiar. I had a breakdown. I questioned God, *Why do we have to lose people we love, why suffer?* I went on a quest to live life to its fullest, and along the way I had fallen and been left defeated, left with more questions. But I've picked myself up and begun to learn.

CHAPTER 6

Off to College, Independence, Spirit

I worked so hard in my last year of high school. A lot of changes were happening at home. Robert moved out with his new girlfriend; to protect her identity, I will call her Krista. Ivan got married and bought a house in a nearby town. I was working hard and planning which college I was going to. This year was bittersweet because I was so involved in my local church. I felt like I was leaving spirit and family behind. I really enjoyed attending, worshiping my God, and prayer groups; Tuesday gatherings were special for me.

My twin sister Leila got engaged and was in a serious relationship. I was in a moment in my life where I thought in the coming months I would be free from chaos, loneliness, abandonment, and lack of love. Stuck in my own mental thoughts was loneliness. I wanted to conquer life beyond measure; I knew there was so much more than the small town of West Chester, Pennsylvania, and beyond Puerto Rico.

September 7, 1996, was the day both my parents packed my car up with all my clothes, books, and necessities for college. It was a day of independence. I felt liberated, happy, over the moon, so to speak. I was elated beyond words. Ivan came over to the house with a business briefcase and notebooks for classes. He wished me the best. My brother Robert and his girlfriend at the time came over with a laundry basket filled with laundry detergent, dish soap, and cleaning products. I was forever thankful to them, because it all sure came in handy. Robert also gave me cash for gas and whatever I needed. I knew at the time that my twin sister was in her own little world. She was in a new relationship and going to school in Florida to be an airline stewardess, and she didn't have time for me then. It was very much understandable; we were growing apart and learning to live separate lives. I was so happy for her, and I knew she was happy for me at the time. We were growing up and going in very different directions in life. My brother Carlos was so sad, but I promised him I would try to come home as much as I could on breaks and holidays. I would only be about three hours away, one state away.

Papi bought me a 1980 Oldsmobile, and I had it packed with all my belongings. I was so ready to leave Pennsylvania and head off to Garret Mountain in upstate New Jersey. I felt light and happy, my heart pounding with excitement and nervousness. We were taking two packed cars on the New Jersey Turnpike; it was the first time I ever drove on a highway alone. But because it was my first time, Papi was my passenger. I said my goodbyes to my siblings, and off we went. In Mama's car were Leila, her fiancé, and Carlos. Papi and I talked the whole way down. As my heart pounded with fear and excitement, I knew this was a new beginning for me. Papi critiqued my driving; I was also humbled and learning, and I wanted to make him happy and comfortable that I could drive on a six-lane highway without trouble. I also wanted him to know that I was going to be OK alone in another state.

After driving two and a half hours, we pulled over along the highway to get gas and to change places. Papi wanted to drive the rest of the way; I was exhausted but still very excited. When I saw the exit for Garret Mountain, my heart started to pound so fast, and my throat felt like I had a knot when I swallowed. Now I began to get scared, and I heard a voice within: "Lizbeth, everything is going to be fine. I'm with you." I became more relaxed as I saw the entrance of Berkeley College School of Business. The campus was beautiful, in the mountains of Paterson, New Jersey. The scenery was breathtaking. From my apartment, you could overlook the town of Paterson. My apartment was across the street from a 7-Eleven, which was nice, and a pay phone. I did not have a cell phone, so it was nice to get to a pay phone when needed. We unloaded my belongs and straightened up my tiny two-bedroom apartment. I was told I would have roommates, but not until my second year. Once we got everything settled, Mama wanted to go to the grocery store, and we filled up my cabinets with lots of canned foods, like spaghetti and meatballs, chicken noodle soup, and peanut butter and jelly. I was not a big eater. So long as I had mayonnaise and ham and cheese, I was good. I was a ninety eight pound five foot one, so it didn't take much for me to feel full. Leila helped me set up my room, and we went to visit family I had never met before.

My dad grew up in the area, so he knew where to go and who all lived where. The only thing I knew at the time was that my grandfather's sister lived nearby, and all of her children were successful in Paterson and throughout the area. So I was very excited to see them; it had been some time since I had. Papi also had cousins he'd grown up with, and the brother of my abuelo (grandpa) who recently had a stroke was living with his daughter Anna, my cousin. She had a sister, Mirabelle. I was so excited to finally be around Papi's family because up until this point I'd only really known Mama's side of the family.

We went to Anna's, and I got to meet her and her three young children. She was half Puerto Rican and half Columbian, and her children all spoke Spanish. They were all adorable and so sweet. Anna was a little stern with her children, and I felt a little comfortable but also awkward around her. She seemed to look me up and down; I felt intimidated. She showed us the room where her dad was. He was my father's uncle, my grandfather's younger brother. When I walked into the room, there was an odor of urine and a heavy odor of someone lying in their own feces. I felt so saddened all of a sudden, an overwhelming sadness, when I looked into my great-uncle Andreas's eyes; I could see he was suffering. I felt his energy; I felt a heaviness all over my body. He had tears coming from the side of his eyes. I knew in my heart he did not want us to see him that way. The last time I saw him had been when I was much younger and visiting Puerto Rico with Papi; he owned a small bodega store where you could buy milk, eggs, bread, liquor—whatever you needed. He was very welcoming back then. Those were the immediate memories I had when I walked in the room. I saw his eyes widen when he saw Carlos; it was as if he were looking at a young version of himself. He was amazed at how much Carlos resembled him and was overwhelmed with tears. Papi rubbed his head and said to him, "We are all praying for you and are happy to see you." Andreas could no longer speak due to the stroke he had suffered. But I know in his heart he was so happy we were there to spend some time with him. This was the first time I had ever seen the effects of what a stroke can do to a person. It was one of the saddest things anyone can witness. Lying in a bed stagnant, unable to speak or to move their body, just watching TV. Anna's grandmother was his caretaker.

I did not get a good vibe or a positive gut feeling from Anna. She was overweight and unwed with three children, and working a school bus driver. As I began to build my own judgments, the energy coming off her was not a good one. I felt a negative energy that came off of her. It was not welcoming, but I completely stayed open-minded. As we sat, Anna called Mirabelle; she was on her way over to the house. It was getting late, and Mama and Papi needed to head back to Pennsylvania before it got later. My car was parked outside; the drive to my apartment was about twenty minutes, but I was unsure of how to get back. I had no phone or GPS; I relied heavily on instinct and intuition. By the time Mirabelle showed up, I felt so welcomed, and such a kind soul she was. She walked in with a beautiful little two-year-old. The little girl's name was Sol; in Spanish this means "sun." She was a bright little girl who could carry a conversation like no other. As my family was getting up to say their goodbyes, I felt an overwhelming sadness. Mirabelle said, "Don't worry, I will make sure she gets back to her place and watch over her; since it's the weekend she can stay at my place." I felt safe and was looking forward to getting to know her. I felt a connection with her.

As I said my goodbyes to Carlos and Leila, Mama and Papi, they all said, "Keep your head up and stay focused. Call us when you can." I was very emotional, but as they were leaving, I got in my car to follow Mirabelle to her house. She spoke very good English but with an accent, so I put my Spanish language to good use. It was very enlightening to speak the language of my heritage and to be around family that I had never known. It was refreshing but scary to be in the unknown.

CHAPTER 7

On My Own, Suffering, Pain

Mirabelle's place was cute, I saw as I parked outside behind her car. We walked up to a large home, but as I entered her place we walked up the stairs to her door; she lived on the second floor of a house in a spacious two-bedroom apartment. She walked me to her daughter's bedroom, which was beautiful with pink-and-white satin sheets. She said Sol didn't sleep in that room; she slept with Mirabelle in her bedroom. The whole apartment was decorated in a supercute way, and tidy. Mirabelle said she was a stay-at-home mommy and that she was not married to her daughter's father because he was married in the Dominican Republic, and that until he got divorced she would not move forward with him. She also opened up and said that while she loved him very much, he took care of all her needs and all of her bills. I was taken aback and thought, *Wow, how do you not work to pay for where you live?* It was strange to me, because I always grew up in a household where both parents worked hard to pay for the house and all necessities. So, in my mind, my thoughts were that Sol's father must be wealthy.

The evening was hard for me as I lay in bed, the room dark and very unknown and out of the norm for me. I cried quietly and alone and asked God if this was the only right decision I had ever made in my life, to choose a college far away from family and anyone that I really had known all my life. I felt a nudge, a warmth that came over me, and a thought of *This is your journey, Lizabeth,* and *Embrace it.*

I woke up the next morning, and I smelled food. Mirabelle was so welcoming and made breakfast for me; it was so thoughtful of her. We both sat down and ate together with Sol, and she said she was going to show me around Paterson and show me how to get from her house to my apartment. I was looking forward to the day; the town was a much larger town than where I came from. I began to feel overwhelmed because all the streets looked the same.

As the days and weeks and months went on, I became very accustomed to my surroundings in a short period of time. I began to enjoy all of my classes in college; all of my classes were large and full of students of all backgrounds. I had a math class in which I did not understand the professor as he spoke. The student next to me was Spanish; her name was Yvette, and she and I became really close. She was born and raised in the area; as I spoke she said I had an accent. I really never realized that I did; she said I sounded southern. "No," I said, "I'm from Pennsylvania, born and raised." She was of Mexican descent, and I was of Puerto Rican descent. We spoke the same language but were very different in culture. After class I would go to her house, and she would offer me lunch. She was such a great and generous hardworking person. At eighteen years of age she was going to school full time and working full time to help her parents move forward in life. She lived in a tiny apartment with two families. Her parents and aunts and children—I had never seen anything like it in my life. But one thing for sure that I saw was that everyone in the household worked and helped each other out. She knew I didn't have my immediate family nearby, so she would come to my apartment often to check on me and bring me food. On days that I couldn't drive to class, she would come by, and I would go to class with her. I noticed that as we got to be really good friends, her sister did not like the relationship we had. I was not Mexican; I was different. As much as I tried to fit in with them, I was not good enough in their presence, according to her sister Rosi.

So I began to distance myself from everyone until the next semester. I befriended a loud and vivacious older lady, Kathy, who was getting a paralegal degree. We had psychology together; she was an optimistic mother of three, forty-seven years old, and African American. She worked full time as a postal worker and was divorced, trying to make it on her own to raise three boys: Pedro, Eric, and Matthew, sixteen, eleven, and five, respectively. They were very neatly dressed, well-mannered, and prayerful boys. Kathy was very articulate; she had a lot of energy and dedicated her time to her boys. She was a good person to go to for prayer and to keep you on your toes when you were struggling in any classes at Berkeley.

After four semesters at Berkeley, I kept in contact with Mirabelle and Anna. They would call me by paging me. I would always run to a pay phone and call and check in with them to see how they were doing. Mirabelle would always call me to see if I wanted to hang out at her place or babysit while she went out with her friends. I would sit at her place and study; classes were beginning to get harder. There was a strict dress code at school, which was business attire. I applied to work at the school computer lab; if anyone needed help in any computer programming class, or just a basic understanding, I would volunteer my time while overseeing the computer lab. I would go to class all day long, then it was off to the lab from 5:00 p.m. to 10:00 p.m. Weekends I would just drive around, go shopping, and get food.

Then I was told two girls would be moving into my apartment to finish their last semester of school. I didn't mind it, so I met two girls, one from Brazil and the other from the nearby area. They had very different personalities; neither one of them drove, so I would drive them to classes until I said, "No more." Gas was not cheap, and at one point I felt like I was being taken advantage of. I really enjoyed working in the lab; I had a routine going. At the same time, I was going to church on Sundays and going to class getting good grades. I was on the dean's list for straight As and keeping a GPA of 3.5. I felt like I was on top of the moon. I didn't like living with other people; it became a nuisance. We all had different schedules, and the bathroom use and my food getting touched or dishes not being cleaned just became horrific, but it was not too long until I was told I would be moved into a larger house with one roommate.

On break I was going to go back home, and I couldn't take off from work, so I decided to stay home. There was a snowstorm coming, so I didn't want to be far from my apartment. My cousin Mirabelle called and asked me to come over to Anna's because they were just hanging out. When I showed up, they were sitting around a table playing cards and drinking. There was a guy there whom Anna introduced me to as her fellow coworker Omar. She drove school buses and he did too. He shook my hand and said, "Wow, you are beautiful." I said, "Thank you." The look on Anna's face was disturbed. I felt very uncomfortable. Mirabelle and Anna were drinking beers. They offered one to me. I drank a beer, and only being twenty I was afraid. But I didn't want to say no. I wanted to fit in with them. They were playing loud music, and two other guys showed up. Anna began to get extremely loud and flirtatious with all the men who were there. I was offered another beer and said to myself, *Why not? I'm not far from my apartment.*

Mirabelle went outside with one of her friends. I needed to use the bathroom. Anna walked away into her bedroom for a brief moment, so I got up and went into the bathroom, and as I was walking in, my left contact fell out and onto the floor. Omar was right behind me and offered to help pick it up. He stood tall; he was well over six feet tall. He startled me in such a way that I felt very uncomfortable. As he was standing behind me, he closed the bathroom door and locked it.

I said with a smirk, "What are you doing?"

He said, "Nothing, I just want to kiss you."

"No way," I said. "I'm good. I'm going home."

He said, "No, don't leave yet. We are just getting to know each other." I felt his hand on the back of my neck, and he bent down and kissed me so hard he bit my tongue.

Meanwhile, I heard a knock on the door from Anna. She was yelling, "Hey, what's going on in there?"

Omar said, "Nothing, helping her find her contact. It fell out."

I opened the door and grabbed my bag and walked outside.

Mirabelle yelled out, "What's wrong, honey?"

I said, "Nothing, I just want to go home."

She looked at me and said, "Oh, Anna just wants to get laid tonight."

I said, "Well, I have class in the morning, so I'm going to go home," without mentioning what just happened inside. I started to walk away. Omar came outside and offered to walk me to my car, which was parked down the street. I was so scared I wanted to say no, but at the same time, I didn't want to make a scene.

As I was opening my door, he stood at the passenger side and said, "Can I get in for a minute, to talk?"

"OK, that's fine. Just for a minute," I said. "I really have to get home, and I had two beers."

He grabbed me by my face, and he kissed me. He held onto my face so hard; he wouldn't let me go. I couldn't breathe; he said, "It's OK. I'm not going to hurt you. Why are you so difficult?"

"I'm not difficult; I just want to go home."

He said, "I'm a nice guy. I'm friends with your cousin. I drive school buses."

I said, "Please get out of my car. I want to go home." As I turned my head, he punched me so hard, I fell back. He lifted me up, threw me in the back seat of my car, tore my shirt off, pulled off my pants, and as I was regaining consciousness he was on top of me, raping me. He punched me again and wrapped his hands around my throat. I couldn't scream; I felt like I was seeing darkness. The pain of him raping me hurt so badly. I felt like I was floating in the air; it was as if I could look down at my own body and could not fight off this monster, and I couldn't take a breath. I tried to scream, "Stop!" as he entered my body with a pleasurable look in his eyes. As the tears came out, he then tried to console me; all I can remember is the laughter and smile on his face while he yelled vulgar words at me as he was penetrating me. I screamed, "Why are you hurting me?"

When he was done, he got out of my car to pull his pants up; as he did that I locked my doors and pulled off so fast. My cousin I knew was nearby, as he worked as a police officer, but if I went to him, my whole family would think it was my fault. I would be judged and criticized. I had nowhere to go and no one to turn to.

I drove to my apartment. My face was swollen and red; I was bleeding inside and out. I ran into my shower with my shirt halfway on and stood there and just cried. I let the water flow over me and cried; I screamed. I didn't know what to do. I was in so much pain. I screamed to God, "Why, why, why…what did I do to deserve this? Why did I go to Anna's house? Why, God, did you let this happen to me?" If I didn't say anything, I would live with the torment for the rest of my life. If I didn't say anything, this man would get away with what he had done to me. When I called Mirabelle, she asked why I didn't call her and tell her. I cried to her, and her words to me were why did I "come on" to him? He was a married man. I assured her I didn't come on to him; he offered to walk me to my car. In no way did I say he could rape me. While I thought she was someone I could talk to, she was last person to sit and listen to what I had to say.

Anna contacted me, and with sheer madness, she said he was her boyfriend. I was so confused; I thought she said he was married. I just knew I had to stay away from both of them. I felt like I was ganged up on, and both did not believe what he had done to me. He also said that if I ever told anyone, he would find me and kill me. So I knew I had to never go back to Anna's or to see my uncle Andreas ever again. I never went back; I stayed away and held what happened to me to myself. I was angry with God. I felt like I was left alone to suffer. Here I was alone in a town without my immediate family, and when I called home I portrayed everything as if it were great. Deep inside I was struggling in dire pain and depression.

CHAPTER 8

Hiding behind Smiles

As time went on, I would sit in my room in the apartment and just cry. It was the quiet and alone moments when I felt as though my life had always been to suffer thus far, and wondered why. I would go to class and go back and shut life out once I left class. I didn't even want to be around people. I just wanted to be left alone. I could no longer trust or believe in anyone who was in front of me.

The semester ended, and it was time for summer break. During this time I was told I would be moved off campus; after moving into a larger house off campus, I was introduced to a roommate, Roxanne, who was from the area. did not drive and relied heavily on me driving her back and forth from classes. I only drove her as much as I could, as we had different schedules. I became less social with people and only left my room when I needed to go to class. Working in the computer lab became extremely hard for me; my roommate would often ask me how I got the job. She began visiting the computer lab and would sit there to watch my every move.

One day, I walked in for work, and she came to me and said, "You no longer work here. I took the position. I went to the dean and asked to replace you." I was lost and confused and did not understand what I did wrong. She complained that I did not volunteer my help to others in the computer lab. I decided to move my room to another part of the house and distance myself from Roxanne. I stayed to myself. I felt like people from all walks of life were against me in many ways. I felt alone and "dumped" by God.

Not hearing from my family in Pennsylvania became a new normal for me, until one evening my brother and his girlfriend, my mother, and my sister came up to visit me. We hung out in my area of the house. I had the master bedroom of the house, which was the largest room of the house—only because I had been in the house the longest. We went out to dinner, and then we came across a small Spanish nightclub that was open. We wanted to listen to Latin music and dance. My brother and I would get on the dance floor and "shine the night away." Salsa dancing was our thing; although we didn't have professional dancing backgrounds, we danced as if we'd had private lessons all of our lives. The lessons were passed down from our parents, generation after generation. Robert was all smiles; my brother had Mama out on the dance floor, and his girlfriend, who is Caucasian, learned some dance moves on the dance floor. While I was not quite twenty-one years old to even get into such a place, I had my college ID on me. The security at the door was a police officer from the area. When he asked for my ID, I told the man I only carried my college ID on me, as we'd just left my apartment, and provided the location, which was close to campus. He seemed to smirk and said, "OK, I'll let you guys in since you are from out of state." We were all treated as celebrities in the area. People could tell we were not from the area by the way we dressed and the way we danced and because they could see a Caucasian in the mix. People looked at my brother and me on the dance floor as a couple. He was a big, tall guy, and I was a short five-foot-one petite who could move to the beats. I had many onlookers and cheers from the crowd, even the security officer at the entrance, who would come by often to greet us and ask if we were OK or needed a drink. At one point he slipped me a glass of soda with a napkin, and written on the napkin were his phone number and badge number. The precinct he worked at was the one my cousin worked at. I immediately looked over at Mama and said, "He works with my cousin." I was left speechless and of course at the moment had to decline his number. I kept the napkin and put it away in my purse. I didn't know what to think at the moment; I was just flattered that someone would give me his phone number. One thing for sure, I knew he was a police officer and felt, *This is the opportunity that I have to speak about what happened to me.*

It was getting late, so we all decided to leave around 10:30 p.m. Mama and Robert had to get on the road; as they said their goodbyes, my brother made sure I was OK and safe, which I was. Leila was sad, but I assured everyone I was OK.

Class in the morning was tough for me. I ran into Kathy and was so happy that I did. I was in so much need of prayer. Kathy knew how to pray with power; I trusted her, and I trusted her connection to God. She immediately knew that something was wrong with me, simply by looking into my eyes. It was time that I be my true self, be authentic, and let people in. There was nothing to hide behind my dark-brown eyes. As I hugged her in the hallway in between classes, I cried like never before. Everyone stopped and looked, wondering what was wrong with me.

Kathy whispered, "Shhhhh…it's OK, baby. It's OK, I'm here."

I said to her as I cried, "I've lost myself, my sense of what I ever wanted in life. I don't think I can continue coming to school."

She said, "No, honey, you must continue. Talk to me, I'm here for you. Come over my house this Saturday, stay the weekend, and come to church with me."

I promised to come by and spend the weekend with her. The rest of my day went on as if I were floating in the air. I sat in the cafeteria with only a water bottle; as I sat I watched everyone come and go. The loudness of the room, the conversations, the laughter—it all became a blur to me. I felt as though I did not belong. I did not fit in with anyone in the room.

The weekend came, and I packed a bag and left for Kathy's house, which was on the other side of Paterson in a small town called Totowa. It was a beautiful location just across from the waterfalls, a soothing and relaxing place. As I pulled up to the house, I saw Kathy's boys run outside to greet me, superexcited that I was going to stay the weekend. Little Matthew adorably asked to get my bag, while Eric was superecstatic and in his comedic way yelled, "Oh no, are you really staying?" He always had something to say that would just bring a smile and make your heart warm. Such beautiful, gifted, well-mannered boys. All three boys looked exactly like Kathy; that was why I believed she cherished them wholeheartedly.

Kathy cooked a really delicious meal; it was the first time I had ever had black-eyed peas with ham hock and collard greens. As I helped cooked Spanish red rice and beans and fried plantains, we chatted, we laughed, and we prayed; we listened to worship music. It was a good evening. I didn't feel threatened, and there was no alcohol, just simply good people around.

The next morning, as everyone got up to get ready for church, Kathy had worship music on. The atmosphere was just remarkable; as Kathy was making breakfast, she explained to me how the church was and the people who attended. She said, "The church has a fairly new pastor of two years. The previous pastor retired, but there are a lot of people from all walks of life."

As I entered the church, the people were all so welcoming, and because the church was a "black" Baptist church, everyone looked at me a little strangely. I was light-skinned with long black hair and obviously Spanish. I didn't look any different from Kathy's kids; their father was Puerto Rican. Overall, it was a great experience to witness the love for God everyone in the church expressed. I felt like new breath had been blown into my life. I had to forgive others and move on, because I had life to live. As I took in the wonderful weekend I had, it was time for me to go back to my place and get ready to finish up with the semester.

CHAPTER 9

Parties, Sex, and Mistrust

Living in housing with other college students, I never knew where I would be moved come the next semester. I was told that five other girls would be moving into the house. Three of the girls were friends of Roxanne. Throughout break, I continued to attend classes just to finish with my degree earlier. During the break most of the girls had done a walk-through to get prepared for the upcoming semester. I enjoyed the peace and quiet until five new students moved into the house. The house was loud, the bathrooms were taken, dishes piled up—it had turned into total chaos. In order for me to handle the disappointments of having more people living in the house, I befriended everyone and got to know the girls; for some it was the first time living away from home and meeting new people. We planned weekend parties and then introduced alcohol into the mix. So here we were, underage drinking and partying in a house owned by the college. The girls would invite everyone and anyone to the parties; one evening it got so out of hand you couldn't walk through the house. There were a few girls not from the school who attended the party. I didn't know most of the people at the party, just one particular guy who attended. One of the girls not from the area wanted to go into my bedroom. I adamantly said, "No!" I sat down on the couch watching everyone who was coming in and out of the house. I met a guy by the name of Jonathan—he went by the name John—who seemed very charismatic and approachable. We sat down and talked all night long about school, about our upbringing and life in general. We both were the same age, and he looked at me as if dazed. I chuckled and asked him if he was OK.

He said, "I never dated a Puerto Rican girl before, ever."

I said, "Well we are not dating."

From that evening on, we became really good friends. John seem to always be around, waiting at my front porch after my last classes. I would get home, and he would be there with ice cream or snacks. I just didn't like that he was a smoker; I couldn't stand the smell of cigarettes. I invited him to go to church with me. The conversation about church, God, and religion did not go well. My feelings toward John became somewhat distant on my part, though not on his. He continued to come every day after my last class of the day, but I just did not have any feelings for him anymore. I felt smothered by someone whom I had no connection with. He had no aspirations for life; he was a drinker and a smoker. I always had questions for him, and he would never commit to answering them. We did not have much in common, and I realized that as he would sit to listen to my history and my past, he had one thing in his mind—when I would agree to sleep with him. I ended our friendship and focused on my classes in college. A week later I heard John was having sex with one of my roommates. I felt disgusted, ashamed, and taken advantage of in the home I resided in. I couldn't believe how girls would have sex just to have sex. I was not brought up like that. I simply would just hide in my room and cry and ask God how I could continue to go through life with so much deceit. Why couldn't people be like me, honest, sincere, and authentic?

The following months I continued to be alone and not hold conversations with anyone. I began to be tested by the world and all of my surroundings; at the same time, I began the quest of searching for authenticity within people I encountered. The parties continued, and I wanted no part in them; I wanted out of the environment. I finished the semester by moving in with Kathy for the last two months of college at Berkeley. It was the best two months of school I had in New Jersey. Kathy was just awesome; she taught me how to stand up for myself and speak my mind. I learned from her that although we came from different backgrounds, we all "bleed the same blood"; we all have ups and downs in life.

As I completed my classes, I decided to go back home to Pennsylvania with careful thought; I did not want to live in my childhood home, and I wanted to continue my education. Mama said she had spoken to her younger sister Dinora, who said I could stay with her while I attended college in the state capital. I felt comfortable because Dinora was also in nursing school and working full time at the time; her daughter, my cousin, was thirteen years old. I felt close to her because she'd lived with us briefly when I was much younger, and she'd also lived fairly close to our house in a small apartment when my little cousin was about two years old. Her father, who would become Dinora's husband, was in prison at the time. Joshua 1:9: "Have I not commanded you? Be strong and courageous. Do not be afraid; do not be discouraged, for the Lord your God will be with you wherever you go." I could watch over her and further my education.

Dinora was married to a past convict who had been in the prison system for drugs. Not everyone in the family spoke highly about him. But to me at the time, he seemed quiet and always kept to himself. So about two months later, I moved from New Jersey to the state capital of Harrisburg. Dinora welcomed me with open arms; after everything I had been through, I felt like *Wow, this could be a turning point in my life.* I was about to turn twenty-one years old in a few months. While Dinora had a two-bedroom house, the upstairs attic had a mattress on the floor and a desk with a computer where I could do class assignments.

Deborah lived about five minutes from Dinora; knowing she had recently moved from West Chester to Harrisburg, I felt comfortable. Although I didn't miss her living in my house when I was home, it just felt good knowing that I knew people close by. I felt certain about the decision to move to Harrisburg with some hesitation. The first week of being there, I went to visit the college but did not have the fifty dollars to pay for the registration and transfer of credits from Berkeley. Wilmer, Dinora's husband, offered to give me a check, so with that I called home to my parents, and Mama said she would be mailing a check back to pay him for helping me at that moment and also thanked him. Personally, I felt very uncomfortable; I thought he did it out of good conscience.

I started my classes at the nearby university, and everything was going very well. Three weeks into my course program, Dinora and her husband seemed to be very different with me; they sat me down in the kitchen and said it was time for me to get a job and help out. I was a little taken aback; I did not touch their food, I would help clean the house, and I always made sure her kitchen was clean. I went out to look for a job at the nearest market and convenience store. I also babysat her daughter so she wouldn't be home alone. And I became a part of the youth group with the church. Philippians 4:6: "Do not be anxious about anything, but in every situation, by prayer and petition, with thanksgiving, present your requests to God."

My safe haven became the church youth group; I would go out for evening gatherings with the youth group. One particular evening I went out, and when I came back, Dinora said Wilmer had gone out and not been back. She said he was on the computer for some time, then on the phone quietly. She confided in me that he seemed to be very different and distant. So I asked her to go on the computer and see what he was searching for; she said, "You know, I don't know much about computers. Can you help me?" I offered my help since I had experience and knowledge from working in the computer lab. What I began to find out was astonishing, and I was taken aback. I told my aunt Dinora he had been chatting with a woman in New York City and made plans to see her. I was able to get an address and phone number. Dinora was somewhat thankful that I was able to attain this information but, at the same time, embarrassed and distraught.

Wilmer was out of the house for about a week and then came back to Dinora. When he did come back, he didn't know how Dinora had found out about his infidelity, but I made sure to keep my distance. The house was so quiet and very uncomfortable; the evenings felt thick in the air, as if I couldn't breathe. The nights were as if a darkness, a thickness, were all around me. I knew Wilmer had thoughts of revenge in some way or another toward me. Dinora's attitude changed toward me, as if I had done something extremely wrong.

CHAPTER 10

Deceit, Lies, Wedding

I did not want to be in the way of Dinora and Wilmer's strange relationship, so I decided to go away with the youth group to a retreat to the Poconos. Being a full-time student, I did not have the funds to pay, so the church paid in full for me, which was a blessing above all blessings. I met so many new people my age and who also had similar aspirations in life. The retreat was unbelievably amazing. I had never felt so close to God in my life; it was humbly distressing from everything I had ever gone through in my life. John 10:10: "The thief comes only to steal and kill and destroy; I have come that they may have life and have it to the full." I felt so light and high-spirited at this retreat; it really changed me within. It helped me understand that everything I had gone through I must let go and forgive in order to move on and grow.

As I got back to Dinora's house, I was superexcited and wanted to share my excitement. My little cousin was happy that I was back, and so Wilmer and Dinora went shopping. I grabbed my cousin and said,

"Let's go hang out at the fair to meet up with the youth to walk the fair and have some popcorn and snacks." As I was leaving in my car with my cousin, Dinora and Wilmer pulled up and asked where we were going. His tone was voice was very strong and with attitude; as I said, "We are going to hang out with the youth group," he said to my cousin, his daughter, "No! Get out of her car; she is not going."

I did not understand what he meant by that, so I pulled off and parked at the fair parking lot and sat there thinking about how Wilmer had spoken to me. I felt strange; I kept thinking and asking, *What did I do or say that would make their attitude change toward me?* So that evening I went home to West Chester and didn't say where I would be going. I went for the weekend and didn't feel like I wanted to go back to their home. I felt very uncomfortable because of the way I was the one who found out where Wilmer went when he committed adultery.

To unwind and not think about what was going on in the state capital, Leila and a couple of our friends all decided to go out salsa dancing, which is one of my favorite things to do. Right across the street from Mama's house, the Italian social club was turned into a nightclub where people from the community would gather and listen and dance to music. This was a place where I felt I could show off my dance moves and forget about everything that was going on around me and within me. There was just something about the salsa music; once you heard it the music livened you up inside. I danced all night long. Leila had gotten engaged to Tito, a Cuban guy from Delaware County, Pennsylvania—he was a riot! He was loud and superfunny.

I had a blast over the weekend and told Mama that I was dreading going back. I knew I had to go back to finish my classes, but living there became unbearable. Dinora would only cook for three, just for her, her daughter, and her husband. She labeled the food in her refrigerator as if I had touched any of it. I was not eating any of their food, nor did I want to; she was not a good cook. It was never like my mother's food.

I began to lose weight and had gotten superfrail; I began having pains in my left side of my stomach. I thought it was simply from not eating. But one thing for sure is that I made sure to drink plenty of water. I couldn't concentrate in class; I started to get very depressed and would just stay in my room until the weekends, when I continued to go home to hang out with Leila. I was free to have fun and meet new people; to me dancing was not doing anything wrong. I was not hurting people, nor did I have any maliciousness toward others in any way. I just wanted to be and do what I wanted without anyone giving me the evil eye.

I went to Wilmington, Delaware, to a club with Leila and a couple of our friends, and I met a guy, Josea. He was a lot of fun, and we danced all over the dance floor. He took a liking to me, but I was not interested in him at first. But everyone around me pushed me to give him a chance. From the first moment we laid eyes on each other, he would not stop calling me or sending me flowers on a weekly basis. It was nice to chat with someone, but once he began to talk about the future and about how women would always cheat or play mental games with him, the conversations would just push me away. The people Josea hung out with were just more fun and interesting; he seemed to be a little immature, and I knew in my heart this friendship/relationship was not going anywhere.

This went on for about three weeks; he bought me a bracelet and said he loved me already. I was a little taken aback and didn't say anything. I grabbed hold of my sister Leila and said, "What does this guy think he's doing?"

She said, "Just be nice and have fun."

At the same time Leila was planning her wedding; there were a lot of things going on. I didn't put too much emphasis on Josea and focused on the wedding with my sister. Leila was planning on getting married on Valentine's Day. The whole family seemed to be involved in some way or the other; it was one of those things that I knew Leila shouldn't be doing, but she needed to figure out for herself if it was the best decision for her. I had foreseen a dramatic end even before the wedding but kept that to myself. I did not want to get involved, only do what I was supposed to do for the wedding.

Leila didn't seem to mind what I had suggested; she was so blindsided by love for this guy. The sad thing about it was that his mother died suddenly and tragically a few months before the wedding. So emotions were running high for everyone in his family. There was a lot of drinking on both parts; Leila and her fiancé were always drinking and then ending up fighting or hurting each other with words. It was very emotional for my twin.

The day of the wedding, Leila didn't seem to be herself; she was very quiet, almost nonexistent. The wedding turned out to be beautiful and a lot of fun. I danced the night away, and it brought out people I had never seen before and people who were not invited. It was very emotional for me; I felt as though I were losing my twin sister. For the first time, I felt really alone. We shared everything, but Leila seem to have everything in order; her husband, on the other hand, needed to cut back on the alcohol.

Just shy of four months after the wedding, there were issues, and Mama seemed to always be in the know about everything that was going on. Mama and Papi were always at their apartment; Leila and Tito did not have any privacy. It was one of the reasons why I chose to not be so close to everyone in the family. It was rumored that Natalia, our aunt, was sexually involved with Leila's husband. I never really knew if it was true or not, but after everything she had done that I'd witnessed, it wouldn't have surprised me.

CHAPTER 11

Separation, Dating, Is This Right?

Leila was adamant that she no longer wanted to be in a marriage with deceit, lies, drugs, and alcohol. She was adamant that she did not want to be in a marriage like the one that she'd witnessed as a young girl with our own father. We went out dancing with our friends; I wanted to go to church with Mama. I had mixed emotions about going out that night; we met up with Josea and a couple of his friends. We went to a nightclub in Wilmington, and I was not dressed to go to a nightclub; it was very hot summer night. I went anyway, and there were so many people there. It was dark and gloomy, and of course Josea asked me to dance to a salsa song to get the dance floor going. I was dancing; Leila and our friends created a half circle and stood around. There were a lot of people at the bar. I wasn't a drinker, but Josea did buy me a beer. It was so cold and so refreshing, with a bitter aftertaste. I thought to myself, *It's superhot in this place, and I'm having a good time.*

As we stood around, I looked to my left and saw Angelo, the guy from West Chester who lived with Sandra. As I looked, I thought to myself, *What is he doing here?* In that moment I grabbed Leila, and we were dancing on the dance floor. As I danced he stood close by and stared and watched us. I was intensely mesmerized by his eyes; he smelled so good I couldn't keep my eyes off of him. As I looked over at him, my heart seem to want to jump out of my chest. As I walked by when the song was over, the next song came on, and he asked me to dance. As we were dancing, he asked for Leila's phone number. I was a little taken aback because I knew the connection I had toward him was overwhelmingly strong. I just felt in my heart, *This is the man I'm going to marry one day.* In that moment I did not care about the relationship he was in or from the past; I had no idea of the circumstances. All I knew 100 percent was that he was not married and did not have any children. I wrote on a piece of paper my name and phone number. Leila in all truthfulness was legitimately still married; I could not put her name on the piece of paper. As I walked away, I immediately told Leila, and she just laughed; we both laughed together.

In that precise moment, a turmoil of chaos began; it seemed that a fight began by the bar. I could not really see what was going on, but people began to run outside. I grabbed ahold of Leila; we held on for dear life and ran out of the parking lot. I looked around for Angelo but could not see him in sight. People were screaming a familiar name; it sounded like Neal, a well-known drug dealer who was originally from West Chester but resided in Wilmington. My heart was pounding so hard; I thought to myself, *Where is Angelo, where is Angelo?* I didn't see him anywhere.

Leila screamed, "Let's get in the car and go home!" Of course I had driven my car, and I was so shaken up and so worried. We talked the whole way home and couldn't believe such an awesome evening dancing had turned into chaos.

The next morning I got a phone call from Angelo, and my heart began to pound and go really fast. I'd known he was going to call; I'd thought about him all night long. I was afraid of what Mama would say; all I heard her say was "Angelo is on the phone."

As I ran to get the phone, I could hear his soft voice say, "How are you?"

I said, "It was a crazy night, how are you?"

Angelo began to say that he was the one who was jumped by several people in the crowd because of something he'd witnessed years ago that was out of his control and something he had nothing to do with; he did not understand why he was hit in the head with brass knuckles from behind. I felt so bad that he was the one who was hit from behind by some thugs; all I could say at the moment was those who were involved "will get theirs in one way or another." I tried to comfort him in any way that I could over the phone.

Angelo said, "I want to see you, can I drive by to see you?"

As my heart started to flitter, I was overjoyed with emotions and said, "Sure, come by. I will be sitting out front of my parents' house." I knew the white Mustang he drove because I had seen the woman he used to live with drive the white Mustang. I was unsure of that relationship at the present moment and did not care, as I knew he'd never wed that woman, and I never saw them together. It was not my problem to figure out the relationship but to go by his word; those were my particular thoughts at the moment. As I heard the car pull up, Leila and I walked up to the car and could see that he had bandages on his forehead and nose, and also he turned his head and had a large bandage on the back of his head.

I immediately felt so sad for him. As I was leaning into his car talking to Angelo, my first question to him was "Are you still with that lady Sandra?" His response to me was at the moment he'd gotten home in the early morning, all of his clothes were packed into plastic bags, and she was told that he was in a fight over a woman. He also was adamant that there was no relationship between them; he had moved into his parents' home. He also mentioned to me he did not want to go back to her, that she was crazy, always fighting with him and many times threatening him with a knife.

I honestly did not care at the moment because they were together for seven years, never getting married, and she had three daughters and two baby daddies. To me there was a reason why they did not get married, and at that moment I did not want to care. I just knew in my heart they were not meant to be, and he was my soul mate. I knew from the very first moment I met him and talked to him; I just knew in my core being this was the man I was going to marry one day.

As we talked about the prior evening, I could see my mother come out to the porch of the house with a broom; as she was sweeping the floors, she looked out and yelled to Angelo, "I know who you are; you are Sandra's husband. I know exactly who you are. I don't want any problems around here. You better leave right now."

As I looked up at my mother, I yelled back at her and screamed, "They are not together, so stop yelling out something you have no idea about!"

She yelled, "He's a no-good son of a bitch! I don't want him around my house, damn it."

He said he would call me later and pulled off.

As I walked into the house, Mama was still screaming, and she said, "I know of him. He is a womanizer, he is no good, and he lives with Sandra."

I told her and assured her he did not live with her anymore; he was living in Delaware at his parents' home.

The next two weeks turned into a lot of phone conversations; I wanted to learn more about Angelo, his past, his present, what he wanted in life. I began to delve deeper and connect with his true self; he had a mysterious look to him. His large eyes were mesmerizing; he had dark, silky black hair; and his demeanor was so gentle yet so masculine.

I made plans with Leila to go into town and hang out with our cousins and friends. There was a Latin nightclub that was open to the public, so I called Angelo to see if he had any plans for the weekend. He asked me what I was going to be doing. I told him I was going to the Star Social Club to have a few drinks and go dancing with my sister and cousins and meet up with some friends. He said he would stop by and see me. I knew he would stop by, so I was ecstatic and so looking forward to simply having fun.

The night started off great, lots of dancing and people coming in; some I enjoyed being around, and some I wished were not there. I kept looking at the clock as I was sitting at the table with Leila and Jazmin; we were talking and having a good ole time watching people dance. As I looked up, I could see Angelo walk in with a familiar guy from the area. I watched him walk in and stand close to the entryway, looking around. My heart started pounding, and I was filled with emotions; we locked eye contact and both smiled at each other.

At the entryway there was a table with two women there. They were related to Eliza; it was her cousin and Eliza's aunt. Eliza's cousin was very well-known in the Puerto Rican community of being very promiscuous with several baby daddies. She grabbed Angelo to dance a salsa song, and he did not refuse. I did not mind; we were not dating. He was just someone I was extremely interested in. As the song was nearly ending, I was walking over to the bar to get a soda, and he grabbed me to dance the next song. As we held hands to dance, I could smell his cologne; he smelled so good, I did not want to let go of him. He asked me what I was going to do after the evening. I asked him what he had in mind. He wanted to go for a ride and talk. I did not hesitate. He said, "We will meet up outside in about an hour," after he left to go out for about ten minutes. No one knew we were establishing a good relationship, and we did not want people to speculate or ruin what we were building. As I saw Angelo walk outside, I knew it was my sign to get ready. I had already told Leila and Jazmin that I would be hanging out with Angelo and that I might or might not go home. I had provided Leila with Angelo's cell phone number so she could get in contact with me. So off I went, and I was the happiest person on earth at the present moment. I felt free and liberated.

    I got in his car, and we drove to the city; we talked and laughed and listened to music. I explained to him I was still in college and had many future plans. He was newly single and in the middle of a battle of homeownership separation, and Sandra also had pushed her youngest daughter onto him as his responsibility. The reality of that was that he was not her biological father, but he felt obligated because he was in her life for seven years. In addition, he was helping her eldest daughter with college. It was a coincidence that Sandra's eldest daughter and I went to school together at one point. I did provide my voice of caution over that situation. The evening went on with a lot of opening up, and clearing the air on both parts was comforting. He asked if I wanted to go home; I certainly did not and neither did he. We enjoyed each other's presence. We booked a room at a nice hotel. It was spontaneous and superexciting. I never thought or asked myself what was I doing or why I was there, or what my family would think of me. I just knew it felt right, and I knew that this was the man I wanted to be with. He was superarticulate, super-romantic, and just very different. He wanted to know me for who I was. It felt so right; we had gotten to know each other, and it felt like we'd known each other for decades.

    Once I got comfortable and settled in the room, we listened to music, we danced, we talked about our future and our families. We compared where our families came from in Puerto Rico. I had future desires but nothing really concrete. I knew I wanted a career, and most importantly I wanted a husband and I wanted to be a mother; I wanted a family. I expressed the emotional and physical abuse I had endured in my life. I told him I felt safe, and I felt really cared about in the moment.

    Angelo looked into my eyes, deep within, and said I never had to worry about anything ever again. He would take care of me. Angelo held me in his arms and just hugged me; he cuddled me like no one had ever done in my life. I felt his cheek pressed up against mine; I turned, and we just kissed and kissed like never before, ever. I'd never felt so wanted and so welcomed by anyone. I told him I never wanted to be apart from him, and he assured me he would take care of me and love me and give me everything I wanted in life.

This evening was the first evening we spent together; the next morning when I went home, Mama was not happy with me. I assured her his relationship with his ex was over, and no one was going to intervene in what I had with Angelo. Papi was not happy that Angelo was ten years older than me; he asked what his intentions were with me. I said, "I'm going to live my life, work, have a family, and most importantly live better than the way I was brought up."

Robert was not happy; he was upstairs the moment Mama was yelling at me. He came down and said, "Sis, what are you doing with that guy? He lives with that lady."

I immediately yelled back at him and said, "They are *not* together! Why is everyone saying crazy stuff that you don't know?"

The following week I moved out and moved with Angelo. I wanted out of the chaos of the house I grew up in and the people I was surrounded by.

CHAPTER 12

Pregnancy, Work Life, Relationship

I had just heard the most exciting news: Leila was pregnant. My heart was thrilled for her; however, she was not happy about this pregnancy, and I felt so sad for her. She was separated from Tito, and she loved her husband, but Mama couldn't seem to stay out of her marriage and let them work on it. I didn't understand the tension, the aggressiveness, or the overbearing nature of Mama's attitude.

I had been inseparable from Angelo; I had not left his side. In fact I'd been staying with him every day and working. He rented a room from a good friend of both of ours, and we both had been working and saving so that we could get our own apartment. It had been four months since we started talking and dating; we now had been staying together. We had so much in common, and our career goals were in alignment; we were strongly compatible. My relationship with my parents had been a little strained because of my trust in my relationship with Angelo. I was stubborn, and I was twenty-one years old, and I knew I was right at this point in my life. Love was stronger than anything in this world at this point, and I wanted to do what I wanted to do and not listen to the naysayers, even those in my past as well as Angelo's past relationship.

But doggone it, what a coincidence that the mother of one of my cousins kept calling Angelo's cell phone. Interesting. I didn't understand, but I did find the opportunity to ask what the heck was going on. As his phone began to ring again and it was certainly my cousin's mother, he said he had a one-night stand with her, and my heart fell to the ground. I knew she was someone who did cocaine and had four children with four different baby daddies; I felt disgusted and awkward. I felt a tingle all over my body, and I was not sure if I wanted to proceed with this relationship. Myself not having a lot of emotional relationships, I questioned and asked God if this was the correct path to take and continue. Then immediately after these thoughts I felt an overwhelming sadness, empathy, and then anger toward this woman and myself for falling for Angelo. Who was I to judge?

In the midst of all this, I fell ill and was not feeling like myself. I had a hard time walking and keeping food down, and had a sharp pain on my left side of my belly, a pain I had felt before, but this time it was severe. Every breath I took or step I tried to take it felt like the wind was trying to knock me over. It got so bad I ended up in the emergency room. As I sat for over an hour before being seen, I was told I would be having blood work and an X-ray done. The results came back shortly after two hours, and I was then taken into emergency surgery for an erupted ovarian cyst on my left ovary. Eight hours later, I woke up so thankful and no longer in pain. I had flowers from Angelo delivered to my room in the hospital. I was happy to have Mama and Papi by my side. I was so happy that I'd paid attention to my body and knew that something was not right, and I sought attention from a medical professional because had I waited any longer my story, my journey would have been written differently.

As my mind wandered, I again began to question God, the source. I began to put my trust to the side of me and distance myself from Angelo emotionally. I really enjoyed being away from my family, but at the same time I wondered if I was doing the right thing at this precise moment in my life. I'd started to really care for Angelo, but I could not say at this point it felt lasting and forever. I had heard many times, "Trust the process," but this was not that feeling. I was just simply living to get by. Every time I felt like it was not a forever relationship, I would always hear a voice within: "He's your soul mate."

My relationship was evolving. I moved to the state of Delaware with Angelo; we found an apartment that was suitable for the both of us, and if we wanted family to stay we had plenty of room. There were also very trying times between Angelo and me. The saying goes, "You really don't know someone until you live with them," and it's very true. I don't know what it was, but early on in our relationship, he felt like he was obligated to continue to take care of Sandra's youngest daughter, and I felt like she merely was just trying to interrupt the beautiful love we had for each other. I continued to pray to God to remove obstacles that were interferences, and sure enough within a couple of months I really made him open up to the child and her mother to explain that although he was not her biological father, he would be there in her life if she needed him. That his life had now moved on with me, who would be his future wife.

It took about five years of trials and tribulations, lies, mistrust, and emotional abuse. I never understood why he wanted to be there for this child who was not his, but he had a child, a son, when he was just eighteen years old who never was a part of his life. The stories I knew were that his ex-girlfriend kept him away from being a father to his own child. I also heard from Angelo's family that his son was raised by his cousin, who married his son's mother and had two other children. He grew up in a two-parent household. Anytime I brought up his son's name, Angelo would get furious with me, as if he wanted me to never bring up a situation I knew nothing about. So for years I kept it at that, and in moments when I would see his son, I made it known that he could come to us for whatever he needed.

The first year of my relationship I felt like I put my family to the side, my future self to the side, my friends to the side for Angelo. He was everything in my life, so I thought in the moment. Until I found bills that he was paying that had nothing to do with us. If I questioned him, he would get very angry with me. His eyes would get so big to the point where he would then leave and not come home until the morning. He would come home with bloodshot red eyes, smelling like alcohol. I would be left alone. This became a weekend ordeal. I would leave and stay with my parents, and he would call me to come home.

I knew that all relationships had problems of their own, but I did not know that this was not supposed to be normal. I did not understand why my heart was in this relationship; my thoughts were always all over the place. When I wanted to leave, I was guided to always come back. What was it? Sometimes when we focus our energy on what we truly want even if we desire to accomplish new things or directions in our life, the energy that you put out and desired the most is accomplished, just not in the direct order of the way you had initially thought.

My brother Robert had broken up with his girlfriend, Krista, and met another girl from the Kennett area. He had brought her over to the house; her name was Krista, too. I couldn't believe it; I was not too fond of her at all, just like he was not fond of Angelo. I had a gut feeling about her, but he was head over heels for her. I didn't have to have a friendship with her, so I didn't care. She seemed to be very different, quiet; something was off. Anyway, it was not my relationship, so I didn't care. I did tell Robert she seemed like someone who had been around; he insisted she was a cool person, so I went along with it because he seemed to care about her.

Within a few months, Robert moved in with Krista; however, she lied to her parents that they were ever living together. So based on that, what else was she capable of lying about? This was something Mama knew, and her whole family. Because of this, everyone in the family had something negative to say about Krista.

A few months later, Robert confided in me that he was given something and needed to see a doctor, and immediately he went to see a doctor and was taken care of. Then within a short period of time, he proposed to Krista. She and I were not superclose; however, I supported him because, well, he was my brother, and I loved him dearly. He was my best friend just as Carlos was, so I went along with them both as they planned their wedding. I'd seen what others in the family did not see: she really loved my brother.

Four days before the wedding, Robert wanted to call off the wedding; he came home to Mama's house and was adamant that it was over, the relationship was done. I felt so bad, because here we were four days away, and she was at Mama's house crying; he'd reacted in a way that I had never seem him before. Robert was angry; as Krista cried and tried to console Robert, he pushed her away so hard she fell back. In a quick reaction, we all ran outside to see what the commotion was all about and tried to calm both down. A lot of people were invited to the wedding, a lot of family and friends. We just wanted them both to understand that we all had problems that could amicably be resolved by talking, not yelling or screaming at one another. The wedding went on as planned; it was absolutely beautiful. I was so emotional and so happy to see my brother at the altar, but something was off, while Robert had a good time dancing and laughing with family. Something was just off, and I felt his energy. All I could ask Robert was "Are you OK?" and as always his response was "I'm good, Sis."

There was a lot that I wanted to confide to my brothers and my sister. I did not want anyone to know what I was going through personally.

I put on a persona and went with it; I just knew the only person who could help me was Jesus. All I needed to do was pray to God to be faithful in his word. I already knew I was living in sin because I'd left my parents' home without getting married. But I knew in my heart that I was going to get married one day and didn't care who was for it or who was against it. I just knew I had to stand in my power and be the best person I could be, my true, authentic self, and continue to be humble.

I was sitting in our apartment living room and heard Angelo walk in. He walked right to the bathroom, and I heard the shower go on. I had cooked dinner, and I could smell the cologne as he walked by. "I'm going out, I'll see you later."

"OK, where are you going?" I asked.

"Out to play some pool."

As much as I didn't want him to leave me, he left anyway. At a mere twenty-one years of age, my focus was not about hanging out with friends; it was all about spending time with someone who appreciated me to the fullest extent as an individual who was not perfect all the time. I was not a crowd pleaser or someone who enjoys large gatherings. I really liked to simply stay home and cuddle in front of a really good movie or TV show. I could not understand the reason behind Angelo's wanting to go out on weekends.

I decided to simply pray to God and leave it in his hands because this was only a phase or a distraction from other people. This was all temporary, but for how long? The future was so unknown; I decided to stay open to the opportunities life had to offer me. I found a job close by, the same location where we attained our automobile insurance. This was my first time in the professional-career world. I was happy, and I began to meet a lot of people in the area. One thing for sure that I began to notice at this particular time in my life were the insecurities Angelo had within himself. He began to question me about my boss's son and did not like the mere fact that I worked around another male.

Five years of relationship schooling was the best experience of my life. Some would say, "Why stay that long without marriage?" There were downs, and there were plenty of ups. We had great experiences before walking down the aisle. I really learned to put God first and then trust daily life experiences. I was open to inner struggles. This is where a lot of people all around the world get stuck. Being open to possibilities, whether good or bad, staying open is when you learn the most about who you really are. Accepting that you have to trust life and situations around you is when you allow the universe to open the door, inch by inch at a time. I did not know that Angelo had planned an engagement, had already spoken to my parents and my siblings to take my hand in marriage. Angelo was so anxious on Valentine's Day the year he proposed to me. I was home ironing clothes in my underwear and bra, and he walked in from work, went down on one knee, and asked me to marry him. He was so nervous yet so anxious he could not wait for dinner to propose. Of course, I immediately said yes! We went to dinner, then went to my parents' house. To my amazement everyone already knew!

Shortly after getting engaged, I became pregnant, and I felt really happy inside and out. Friends and family always commented about the glow I had, but my inner thoughts were the word *trust* again and again. Not everyone was happy that I was pregnant, and some may have wished that I would not be pregnant. It was a trying time for me; I felt sick a lot, and everything smelled. OK, it might have been normal to some, but it was brand-new to me. I began to put on weight, and Angelo did not seem to be happy. Rather he spent a lot of time with the daughter of his ex-girlfriend, which was fine; she was ten years old and needed the affection of a father figure in her life. I began to retain a lot of fluid in my body, and the baby's heartbeat during appointments was not as strong. Angelo was not so involved in my pregnancy; he was working a lot and always had weekend plans with the "daughter" who was not his biologically. I felt like I was put on the back burner; it was not the relationship I had dreamed of, but I knew it was temporary.

I started to bleed when I went to the bathroom and did not think it was anything to worry because it was just a spot. Only when I began to have really bad pains did I begin to worry. I went to the doctor and was sent to get an ultrasound, where I was told the baby had abnormalities and no heartbeat. I still had to deliver my baby and go home empty; I felt a total loss. I was angry at everyone around me and God.

We all go through life expecting to have nothing but positivity, hoping for the best, hoping we get what we want all the time. We are human; it is expected that if we do the right things in life, we should have everything come our way with no problems. Easily said—if that were the case, life would be easy; it is through the challenges and experiences we go through in life that we find the lesson. What did I do to cause my baby that I wanted so bad in the world to die? Then I began to think of everything I have ever said negatively to hurt someone, and I also wondered if I was a disrespectful child of God toward my parents in any way, shape, or form. I cannot judge myself, but what can I learn? The only person I have ever hurt was myself.

Going back four months into my relationship with Angelo, I had become pregnant, and with the uncertainty of my relationship, I'd had an abortion at the nearest Planned Parenthood. It was the most traumatizing experience I had ever gone through in my life. It was a decision that we both decided: yes, we wanted to be together, but his mind was already made up because in his mind he was taking care of his "daughter," which I knew did not make any sense; he had no daughter, but out of anger I went ahead and had the abortion. My parents did not know, nor did I want them to know because of my upbringing; having a baby before marriage would have hurt my father. So was I being punished for what I had done? How could I get rid of a blessing that so many have a hard time achieving? I had to learn how to cope with what I had done and answer to God, the universe, and my internal thoughts. Now I was confronted with the loss of the baby I so dearly wanted to have in my life.

CHAPTER 13

Stress, Family Gossip, Forward Movement

Losing my baby was the hardest experience I had endured. Watching Leila give birth to her son was a miracle. Knowing everything she had gone through with her failed marriage, I knew in my heart I did not want to experience what she had gone through. I wanted to devote my time to nurturing my body back to health. I knew in my heart that God had a purpose for me; my baby had had congenital heart failure and also had the chromosomes of Down syndrome, and while I was angry, lost, and confused as to what had happened, I knew that one day I would see my baby in heaven. I also knew that I would be a mommy one day; it was not up to me at that time.

I also wanted to work on my relationship with Angelo without the added outside distractions from family on both sides. No more distractions with his ex and her daughter. All barriers were cut, and we focused on our growth as a couple, two people who needed to simply just share the love with one another. We enjoyed our engagement and life together. I needed to learn how to be my own person, not be told how to live by both my mother and Angelo's mother. Each had her own way of life and wanted to instill her own way of doing or accomplishing daily life, like how to cook and what to cook for Angelo, but I needed to find my own way.

The moment I thought I could breathe is when more turmoil began to build up. The constant gossip with Angelo's family continued to boil over the reason behind the death of my baby as to who or the reason at fault. Receiving no encouragement or sympathy whatsoever, I was questioned over and over again by Angelo's mother. I never felt welcomed by any of his family members until then. I did not feel comfortable building a relationship with them because they were, of course, all older than myself, and I always felt some form of intimidation, threatened in some way. I began to feel comfortable around his younger sister Malinda. She was about six years older than myself. We had similar likes, and to this day I don't know if the relationship was ever been sincere..

After going through losing my baby and my relationship being tested, now I endured family gossip from my mother's sisters. My mother was one of seven sisters and four brothers. One of each at this point had passed, the two whom I most adored in this world. Nonetheless, gossip had always been a factor in my upbringing, from family members on my mother's side. It seem like none of Mama's sisters were supersuccessful or had anything of their own. Every single one of them at some time or another had lived in my childhood home. All endured a troubled past in some way or another, from devious lies to imprisonment, gossip, assault, drugs, and theft. Like many families in the Puerto Rican culture and around the world, there are members of the family who are estranged; I never really understood why, until adulthood. There seemed to always be a shift of some sort in my life and what I realized around me through the years.

The moment when I learned to let go of past experiences and trust my relationship with Angelo, my life fell into place. I began to distance myself from my own family, my siblings, cousins, aunt, and uncles; and Angelo did not have a close, tight-knit relationship with his siblings, so that in itself was not questionable. We both simply began to focus on our goals and our relationship. I admit I love my siblings, but as we were getting older and living our own separate lives, we continued to stay in communication by way of a weekly phone call or text check-in. The one thing that no one could take from me was the relationship I had with my siblings. I could never understand or never wanted to understand why Angelo did not have a close relationship with his siblings. Every time I tried to ask about any one of his siblings, he always seemed to brush it off. In my opinion it was not my place to question him or ask his parents about the odd relationship, if any there was. To my amusement, his parents always seemed to relate as though all of their children had a wonderful relationship growing up into adulthood. This was not what I witnessed or observed through the relationship I had with Angelo. I just knew that in the weeks and months coming near, I would see for myself the relationship Angelo had with his family.

As we both continued to work and build our life together despite the trials and tribulations of change and intermittent distractions from outside sources, we did what any ordinary couple did: work to pay bills, put a roof over our heads, make sure we had a nice home to go to. The insecurities never diminished fully; however, we began to trust the process of what I call "life." This living arrangement did not go without issues in the relationship, as Angelo continued to go out on the weekends, make plans without me, drink, and hang out with his friends. I had a journey of my own, to really find myself in the mist of all the chaos of what was to be lived and learned.

CHAPTER 14

Pregnancy, Sickness, Alone

I was home with Mama and Leila at the house; it was a Friday night, and I decided to stay. I was not feeling like myself; the smell of beans made my stomach turn. I thought I was coming down with the flu, as my stomach was so upset and my throat was scratchy and irritated. Leila decided to go to CVS and buy a pregnancy test. As she ran to the store, I went to lie in Mama's bed and rest. Leila was back from the store within fifteen minutes and shook me out of the bed to take the pregnancy test. To my amazement one purple line meant not pregnant, and two purple lines meant pregnant. The test stated to wait at least five minutes; within two minutes the test showed positive for pregnancy. I felt an overwhelming tingle all over my body, an excitement that was hard to explain. I felt faint, as if I were having an out-of-body experience, and knew in my heart that I would have a son.

As Leila and I ran down stairs to share the news with Mama and Papi, Mama's reaction was "You better call Angelo," and I knew he was out with his friends. My plans were to stay with Mama, as I called him and advised him to come to the house. He showed up within the hour and asked me if I was going to come home. I initially said no, but with excitement I had to show him the test. I'm not so sure he took the news with excitement, but rather with curiosity, amazement, worry, and enthusiasm. As we spoke about what was next, my first reaction was to let him know that I would be moving to Mama's until the baby was born. His reaction was not what I had expected at that precise moment but one that questioned our relationship as a couple. I did not know what the future held for us as a couple; I just knew we loved each other, and we were going to work on our relationship together with love.

The drinking and late nights out on the weekends did not stop, so I decided to pack my things up and move in with Mama; considering my previous pregnancy and loss, my main focus was to have a healthy pregnancy and a healthy baby at all costs. I continued to work full time and take care of myself. Everything was going smoothly until early spring 2001; Mama was on vacation visiting her sister in Florida with Leila. I was alone with Papi at the house and not feeling very well. I felt weak, nauseous, could not keep food down, and did not have the energy to drink anything. So I immediately went to the doctor, and due to previous circumstances I was sent to the hospital for observation. Angelo was unaware of my condition; he was out entertaining the daughter of his ex. I felt alone and scared, but I began to pray to God to watch over my health. I was diagnosed with hyperemesis, a condition in the early pregnancy that disturbs electrolytes and causes extreme nausea and weight loss that can lead to dehydration; it can last well into fourteen to twenty weeks of pregnancy. I spent a whole week in the hospital, alone and sad; it was a time to reflect on what I needed to focus on, and it was solely my baby.

Once I returned home from the hospital, I continued to work well into a week before birth. One September 11, 2001, I woke up not feeling like myself; I was feeling nauseous and drained. I did not know my job had a planned baby shower, and at the same time I remember getting up out of bed with my big belly and going downstairs to watch the news of a plane hitting the Twin Towers. It was devastating news, and at the same time I got a call from work: my coworkers were bringing all my gifts from my shower to my house.

My due date was initially December 22, but I went into the hospital the morning of December 10, 2001; my son planned on trying to stay a little longer, as he turned breach on me, and I had two doctors who tried to turn his little body as he lay in my belly. It was such a surreal experience of nervousness and anxiety, my heart beating fast in anticipation of what this little guy would look like. Due to my blood pressure rising and his heart rate lowering, I was sent to the operating room for emergency C-section. Angelo was the only one allowed in the surgical room, which was very comforting. As the doctors prepared for the delivery of our son Matthew, my brother Robert and Krista had welcomed my nephew just two days before, such a beautiful experience and so exciting for my happy brother Robert and Krista; he was glowing with excitement. As the both of them walked by my room with baby in hand, I was sad I could not stand up to kiss my little nephew but so excited that our children would grow up together as cousins. Robert walked by my room to give me a kiss on my forehead as he always did. He said with excitement, "I will be back to see you later." As the two walked out of my room, I began to shake with nerves and became overwhelmed with so many emotions and anticipation in wanting to meet Matthew, the little human being who had been moving around in my belly, for the very first time.

Dr. Curry and an intern from Europe began my C-section. The beeping monitors were loud, the lights were bright, and the energy in the room was thick, strong, light, and airy, as if I had so many people around me; yet at one point everything went silent, and then I heard the loud cry of a newborn baby. I looked up, stared into Matthew's big, dark eyes, and thought, *Wow, he looks so much like* me. The nurse gently positioned Matthew against my cheek. He was adorable and tiny with round, chubby cheeks and a loud cry that could be heard down the hall. While initially Angelo was sitting next to me, he went off to be with Matthew. I was overcome with so many emotions, tears of joy, worry, and excitement! It was the best day of my life, the day I became a mommy, a day I had prayed for, a day God, the universe, and my angel guides were with me. A day I knew and felt in my heart that Grandmom was with me.

In times of the unknown, we often think that no one is with us as we prepare to go through the unknown, unforeseen future. The moment we let go of the obstacles of our own thought, such as the ego (which stands for "edging God out"), the future becomes what we always initially thought about. The process becomes as planned, as it was meant to be. I wanted my son Matthew so badly, I wanted to be a mommy, but I wanted his birth and delivery to be in God's timing. As it was, that was why I named him Matthew, the meaning of which is "the gift of God," and he sure was and always will be. As all children are—the precious gift of God.

CHAPTER 15

I'm a Mom, Marriage, "Papa"

I was over the moon with my little baby boy, just when I thought I was so in love with Angelo; to bring into this world and be blessed by God to have the honor of being a mommy to this bundle of joy was a miracle. Matthew, so tiny, so adorable—I enjoyed smelling his little body, his face, his tiny mouth up against my nose; his little, tiny, squirmy baby voice just made my heart melt.

This was our first experience as parents, and the journey was amazing. Everyone in my family was so excited to meet Matthew; visitation was nonstop at the hospital. I was not sure about nursing Matthew, but I did give it a try and really enjoyed the bonding experience I had with Matthew. He depended on me to eat, and I depended on Angelo for emotional support; he was there by my side every step of the way, every minute, every hour. He was so loving, so gentle; I was so in love. I never thought I could love anyone else, or perhaps an additional person. But as I lay in the hospital bed, just as God loved the world, I, too, could spread the love I had for Angelo and love Matthew so much more. He was a reflection of the love we had for one another.

No one from Angelo's family stopped by to see Matthew when he was born. I had my whole family by my side, and that was very important to me. I was in the hospital for five days recuperating from the Cesarean section, and after an overwhelming time of visitation of family and friends, it was time to go home and start my life as a new mom.

It was not until Matthew was about one month old that Angelo went to take him to meet his grandparents, and family. My emotions were all over the place after having Matthew. I never really focused or paid attention to how fast I drove a car or how I spoke to people, or really appreciated what life had to offer until I delivered Matthew. It was a feeling of oneness, a feeling of authentic love, a feeling of awareness of the new life that had no knowledge of what was yet to be learned. I knew I had a responsibility to be a good mother and teacher, to be emotionally sound, to express good judgment, to teach good morals, and to create a strong, God-loving parental household for Matthew to live in.

Angelo and I moved to a small, two-bedroom home in the serene woods of Chester County. I went back to work when Matthew was just about two months old; it was the hardest decision I had ever made, because I was nursing Matthew, and leaving him in day care was so hard for me. I felt the emotions of abandonment; I felt like I was a bad mother to choose work obligations over the safety and welfare of my baby. I wanted to be home with him so badly; going to work daily was hard for me. A lot with my body and emotions changed; the work atmosphere was not the same for me. I had a responsibility now; I had a yearning to work hard and save up so that I could be home to raise my son. Matthew being in day care as an infant was not easy; he became very ill. At two months old, he became so ill that he was taken to the hospital with trouble breathing and was diagnosed with asthma and colic. He needed a breathing machine just to help his little body rest easy, and round-the-clock care. Life became exhausting, but I pulled through the daily triumphs of motherhood.

When life throws a curve ball, the ball itself can hurt. As I focused so much on Matthew, Angelo continued to lie to me about his visits with the daughter of his ex-girlfriend. The lack of his presence with his own son began to trouble my thoughts. The relationship bothered me in the sense that here I had his biological son, his blood, a child we made out of love, and he was spending his unnecessary time with a child that was not his by his own doing but because his ex-girlfriend was obligating him to do so. It was a distraction in my life that was a negative effect; as I tried to ignore these people in my life, it seemed they continued to stalk me in trying to hurt me and my relationship with Angelo. I wanted to protect Matthew, a tiny, little infant not understanding the trials of life, unknowing of how cruel people could be, at all costs. I did give Angelo an ultimatum: to step up and be a father and husband to me or leave my life for good. I did not want the distractions of his ex-girlfriend or her family in my life. I wanted them to leave me alone so that I could raise my son in peace.

From that moment on, we planned our wedding, we had counseling together as a couple, and we got to know each other so much more profoundly. Sometimes when we let go of what bothers us internally, we begin to understand that there is someone so dear and so close that guides us along the way. The two of us sat down and wrote a list of who we wanted to take part in our wedding. We both wanted people who had been a part of our relationship as a couple; We wanted those who were invited to share our special day. It took months of planning and saving while raising Matthew. Observing his first words and his first steps was amazing to say the least. I spent more time with him, so I thought his first word would be *mama*; unfortunately his first word was *papa*! Matthew would always jump up for joy when Angelo got home from work. He was our pride and joy, made us laugh, and was such a bundle of joy since being born into this world. It was a privilege to be chosen as his parents.

When it came time for our wedding rehearsal, Matthew was about fifteen months old and walking. It was suggested that he would wear a tiny tuxedo and be a part of the wedding. While Angelo and I were already married, it wouldn't be official until I walked down the aisle and shared with close family and friends. Both sets of our parents had to attend the rehearsal along with those who were part of the bridal party. My parents had attended a meeting with the priest who was going to officiate the wedding; the meeting the previous week went very well. While the priest was not able to have a meeting with Angelo's parents after the rehearsal, the Priest sat down with both Angelo's parents. My soon-to-be father-in-law in his gentleness was very happy for both of us. Angelo's mother, on the other hand, seemed to have an attitude during the whole rehearsal. She did not like the fact that we were getting married and wanted to be in control of everything. She had not believed that Matthew was her grandchild until just recently. How could anyone deny it? He looked just like Angelo. I remember when I was about seven and a half months pregnant, she had called looking for Angelo and asked me if I was really sure that the baby I was carrying was in fact his baby. She said no one in the family has ever lost a baby before, that it did not happen within the family. She wanted to know what had happened to the baby I previously lost, why the baby died. I felt humiliated, I was angry, and my internal thoughts were *I don't owe her or anyone any explanations*. I told her over the phone that the baby I was carrying was indeed her son's baby. I was not the type of person to sleep around. I left that conversation at that and said I would let her son know she'd called.

As I looked over at Father Forlano, I could see his face was red and flushed, and I knew for sure Angelo's mother did not approve of our wedding or marriage. I knew in my heart I had to just simply let it go; Angelo was marrying me, not his mother. If she were a better mother to him, he would not have gone through the many ordeals he had personally told me about in his past. Those dear things I kept to myself and never addressed with her, as it was never my business to do so. The rehearsal ended with everyone knowing their place in line; my family left happy, and off we all went to the rehearsal dinner.

Angelo and I decided that we would not spend the night before our wedding together but would rather spend it apart to reflect on our relationship and think about all the counseling we'd had. We had gone through a lot together as a couple; we overcame some issues, but those issues I buried deep within my thoughts, never to bring them back up. We talked the night before; we also exchanged a gift in the morning, a watch we both got each other, and we were very happy with whom we had chosen to take part in the wedding. All my brothers were a part of the bridal party, along with my sister and Angelo sisters-in-law, and Angelo's father was his best man. One of Angelo's sisters was one of my bridesmaids; she was the middle sister who had really accepted me into the family when I first met Angelo. We got along very well, and her husband was one of the lead singers who performed at my Sweet Fifteen years ago. "Small world," as my parents would put it. I always say the universe, God, and Mother Earth put us in situations and places that in many instances we revisit different times in our life. Paying attention to our surrounding is key in the present moment. Living in the present is a reflection of our past thought patterns. People and places we have encountered during our life journey seem to appear again at different times in the near future.

The day was absolutely beautiful; while it rained very hard in the morning as I got ready, the rain stopped as we drove off to the church. Walking down the aisle with both my parents was an amazing idea, the idea I thought and chose with love. I could not walk down the aisle with just my father; I wanted both my parents, as they both together as parents helped raise me. The church I chose was a church where I as an infant was baptized; it was a place where I felt safe and close with God. As the pianist played "Canon in D," I held in hand with my parents. I could not hold back my emotions as I thought of how far I'd come with Angelo in my life. Now we were both parents to Matthew and were about to express our love for one another in front of friends and family. I began to cry tears of happiness and love, looking around as the music just echoed at the dark oak wood, beautiful stained-glass windows, tall ceilings, and large cross with Jesus. I really felt it was totally meant to be. I was not the perfect child, I did have my faults, but I was the best soul having a human experience in the best way I could. I did not invite everyone from my mother's side of the family, those who had treated me unfairly or disrespected me or were there for Angelo and me. I knew there would be talk about me and about us as a couple. I wanted my day to be about me and only me, without issues or problems or gossip. So I decided to only invite two of my mother's sisters to my wedding. The moment we walked out of the church as husband and wife, the sun came out and shone brightly. Up to this point, every detail of the wedding went on as I had planned.

Walking into the wedding reception was absolutely wonderful; I could feel the energy of the room, a lot of love, a lot of wonder and anticipation of what was to come. It was one of the best days of my life, but one with a lot of hesitation and worry. I was not really sure if I had made the best decision. I just knew it was a right decision because Angelo was the father of my child. I wanted Matthew to grow up with both parents.

As our names were called when we entered the reception as Mr. and Mrs., it was a little overwhelming. I could feel my heart beat fast; at this point I wanted to hurry and get it over with because I was just so hungry. Seeing all of my family and friends was exciting; I wanted to talk to all of my guests. We sat at the head table, and we opened up with prayer and dinner. As we ate dinner, the first words out of Angelo's mouth were "What are you looking at?" I put on a fake smile and looked down at my plate and away from everyone so no one would notice I was embarrassed by the way he was talking to me. My internal thoughts were *Why is he talking to me that way? What has gotten into him? I'm not understanding this.* Angelo

Angelo's cousin was the DJ for our wedding reception and to my knowledge did a good job at introducing everyone in the wedding party, as well as making everyone comfortable and making things enjoyable for everyone. I had known his cousin for years, but because I'd known him for years I was not allowed to speak to him or make eye contact with any man in the room. Angelo was going in and out of the reception area to our hotel room, and his demeanor was changing, along with the amount of alcohol he was consuming. I did not understand it, but I did not like how I was being talked to and treated. By the end of the night, Matthew was needing my attention; he was bottle-fed, and I also had to take time out to nurse him. So I took a little time while everyone was dancing to get some rest in my hotel suite and get Matthew to sleep; then I came back down and danced with my brother, my uncle, and my sister. We did the dollar dance. The wedding turned out to be amazing, other than the way Angelo was talking to me behind everyone. No one knew how I was being treated; I put on a fake persona.

The next morning Angelo and I along with Matthew traveled to Puerto Rico for our honeymoon/vacation. Thank goodness Leila was available to drive us to the airport; I knew she had drunk a little too much at my wedding. She was fine, thank goodness. She looked into my eyes and noticed something; she asked me, "Are you OK, Sis?"

I said, "Yes, just supertired." It was a time to travel around the island, visit family, and take in the fresh air of Puerto Rico and reflect on our culture and history.

As little girls, some of us grow up and play with our baby dolls or dolls that were given to us as children. Most move on to the Barbie doll and dream of a fairy-tale wedding after college. Or perhaps some of us focus on our childhood sports and aspire to be the best into adulthood. We never dream or realize the potential ups and downs, the heartaches that we could face. No one ever talks about what could happen, the what-ifs and all the misunderstandings, miscommunications, and mistrust. No one ever knows for sure what is to come. However, I always had the internal thoughts from my God, whom I always prayed to, providing a nudge within my gut. I always had a gut feeling when something was off; I just knew. When you have that feeling, always pay attention because it is your intuition of knowing what is to come and how to either overcome or conquer the negative aspects of what we call life. You can always turn it into a smile instead of a damper so you can continue to keep shining and smiling. What happened was that I did not listen; I believed in God so much, but feeling alone in my own mental thoughts, I let ego lead my life and did not utilize my intuition. I ignored it to feed the flesh; I will go further and explain later.

CHAPTER 16

Married Life, Test, Move

The responsibility of being a wife and full-time working mother was not an easy one. At times I felt like I could not handle it, but the moments when I thought I could not handle it my mind would think of the prayers I had asked of God. My life was going according to what I had initially asked God for, so why was I doubting myself as a wife and mother? I needed to pray to God and ask for forgiveness for the thoughts of doubt and insignificance. God, the universe, does not give you what you cannot handle. I had to pick myself up and keep moving forward.

My life was challenging. The alcohol did not stop, nor did my own insecurities about being simply happy. As Matthew started walking, we decided we needed a larger home. I was still working hard, Angelo was working hard, and we needed more room for Matthew to run around. Our home was a tiny two-bedroom, and if we wanted to have more children, there was not enough space to expand. A family friend's cousin had a home nearby with three bedrooms and offered us to rent it for a reasonable amount, so we went forward and moved in. In between moving we had found out that I was expecting, and Matthew would have a sibling. I knew in my heart that I wanted to have another sibling for Matthew.

When I found out I was expecting my second child, it was a surreal experience. Three months prior Angelo and I had lost another baby. I was already twenty-four weeks along and thought everything was going as expected. The doctor's visits were good, nothing out of the ordinary other than the difference in subtle movements. I did not feel as much as I had when I was pregnant with Matthew. He was very active in my belly with strong kicks; the movements were so strong, I could actually feel my belly look like a mountaintop when lying down. A beautiful experience, to say the least. One evening after work, as I was preparing dinner, I went to the bathroom when I felt a sudden urgency of needing to do a bowel movement, and all of a sudden there was blood in the toilet, and I knew in my heart that something was wrong. Immediately I went to the emergency room, leaving Matthew with Angelo. As I entered the ER, I was told to sit in a wheelchair. I told them I had a sanitary napkin and was bleeding with some pain, but it was tolerable. The doctor came to me and drew some blood, then wheeled me to get an ultrasound. As I lay on the bed, I felt a sudden sadness; my heart was beating fast, and I felt a warmth all over my body. The technician started to run this small imaging piece around my belly and was taking pictures and looking at measurements; then she turned a button on the monitor, and I could hear nothing but static air similar to ocean waves. As she turned the monitor, she said, "OK, we will have to do an internal ultrasound." As soon as she inserted the instrument, I felt pain. I knew the baby was disconnected from me. She said, "I'm so sorry, there is no heartbeat. I will have the doctor discuss the findings with you." I just broke down and cried, feeling hopelessness and so many emotions as to *Why, what did I do so wrong? I'm a young, strong twenty-seven-year-old; this should not happen to me.*

Immediately after talking to the doctor, I was taken into surgery for a D&C to expand the uterine lining / cervix area to remove the baby and allow for genetic testing. I did have some discomfort after surgery. I was heartbroken and sad, but on another note Matthew made me strong. He helped me get through the sadness. He brought me so much joy and laughter that when I did get sad, I would think of how blessed I was to have him and Angelo in my life.

While Angelo was home caring for Matthew, Robert and Mama stayed with me in the hospital until I was discharged. Robert gave me so much comfort, as he said Matt had Brody to play with and that I would be fine. As my big brother, he gave me so much comfort by saying I was young, I could still have children. It was just not meant to be at the precise moment.

He was so right; Matthew was a handful at that time. I was not really ready, but three months later, almost four months, I found out I was expecting my second child. This time, I had stopped working to get my health on track and focus on taking care of Matthew. I wanted to prepare him for kindergarten and get him intellectually ready for reading and writing. Angelo was determined to work hard and allow me to stay home to raise Matthew and focus on my pregnancy. Angelo did not want me to worry or stress; he had his uncle and aunt help us move into our new place. This townhouse was really big, three bedrooms, the perfect size for our growing family. Matthew had so much room to run around; right outside of the door to the left was a small park for him with a couple of swings and a sliding board. There were several young families in the neighborhood, and we were in close proximity to my parents' home and local grocery stores.

I was really enjoying my pregnancy this time around; everywhere I went, people said I glowed, and my belly was growing differently, smaller and rounder. I didn't gain much weight, not as much as when I carried Matthew; I recall I had gained about thirty-five pounds. This time it was less than fifteen pounds, and I was more fit. No morning sickness, no swelling, just enjoying the internal movements of this baby inside of me. The time came when I was able to schedule an ultrasound to determine the sex of the baby, but on the day the baby's legs were crossed. As much as I tried to change positions, the technician was unsuccessful. I already knew from the moment I found out I was expecting that I would have a little girl. I felt it in my soul that I would become a parent of two children, a son and then a daughter. It was the gut feeling, the simply knowing that God was blessing me with a daughter, a little girl just like me.

It was not until my thirty-seventh week of pregnancy when I scheduled a three-dimensional ultrasound that I found out what Angelo and I were going to bring into this world. Papi and Mama; Leila, my twin, and her son, my wonderful nephew; Matthew; and Angelo were together. It was a special moment and one of the happiest ones in my life. As my heart raced, the technician began to rub my belly with some kind of Doppler, and instantaneously we began to see color, the face of the baby as if the baby were looking at us, as if he or she were startled; then we heard hiccups when the sound was turned up. It was a miraculous moment. I could feel a presence in the room, I could feel love, I could feel light and airy as if God were standing next to me. The technician looked at me and asked, "Are you ready to know what you are having?" Without hesitation I began to cry; she said immediately, "You are having a girl." We all started to cheer with excitement; Matthew was so happy for a baby sister. At that very moment, I felt complete and so thankful to God. I knew, I just knew that Titi Nancy was around me. I felt her energy and smelled the scent of the perfume that she used to wear, Exclamation. I felt an overwhelming happiness and sadness that she was not here in the physical to witness me having my children, though I knew in spirit she was.

We were in awe at seeing my little girl's face; it was so beautiful and so similar to Matthew's little face. I could actually see the resemblance to her father. I was so in love and ready for her; however, she was not ready until full term. It was OK; I wanted to enjoy this pregnancy until she was ready to be born. From the moment I left the ultrasound, I began to thank God so much more on a deeper level. I felt the love deep within my soul, but also I began to question my ability to love another human being. I knew that God loves so many, so I knew this was going to be a challenge but one that I too could conquer because she was my flesh; she was designed by love, and I was chosen to be her mama.

Along with the feeling of happiness and enjoyment, I was faced with uncertainty of my future outcome with my family. I went to see my gynecologist for a weekly checkup, and the doctor felt a lump on my left breast that seemed to be concerning. Dr. Acts did an aspiration of the left breast; after two days the results were not good. This far in my pregnancy, it was a concern for the doctor, who requested that I see a surgeon for a second opinion. The lump was behind the milk duct; the size and shape of the cyst was a concern, and the only way to know for sure was to go in and remove it. At the same time I had a black mole on my neck that I'd had for years; it was the mole that family and friends always used to identify my twin sister and myself. I'd heard of others removing moles, but I never knew that sometimes moles could be cancerous. Trusting in the doctor, I removed the mole, though I wished I had not removed it. I felt it was a part of me; I'd had the mole all my life. Then I had surgery to go in and have a lumpectomy done on my left breast; it was a risky surgery because I was pregnant, and going under was a scary moment for me. I did not want to wait until after the baby was born; I needed to know if this was a cancerous cyst or not. Whatever it was I wanted it out of my body. I was not going to allow any obstacle take me down; I was facing everything and anything head-on and pushing forward.

Often we find ourselves questioning every decision we make or have made with the understanding that we always make the right decisions in life. We often don't quite understand what is coming next in our life, what obstacles we will face; we often pray for desires and things we want in life to come to fruition, and we tend to lose faith because we hit many blocks. We hit peaks; these are small messages from the universe and from God that what we desire with a pure heart will come. We have to hold onto the faith and not lose sight. It is when we lose sight of our desires, our hopes, and our dreams that we are tested to see if they are truly what we desire in our life.

CHAPTER 17

Baby, Postpartum, Faith

Graciela came into this world needing a little push to hear her voice; Mama next to me watching her birth was an amazing feeling. Angelo and Leila were just outside the surgical room waiting in anticipation. Angelo wanted my mom to experience her daughter giving birth and watch her granddaughter being born into this world. Graciela was absolutely beautiful, just like the three-dimensional photo that was taken of her prior to being born. She had a lot of hair, her skin was pale and pearly, and her face was round just like her daddy's.

After the excitement of her delivery into this world, I was left alone in the recovery room to reflect on my life. I was not in any pain, but an overwhelming feeling of helpless, incapable, unqualified thoughts came to me. I began to wonder, *I'm now a wife and a mother of a bright little boy and now the mother of a beautiful little girl that Angelo and I both wanted so dearly.* As I lay alone in the recovery room, a nurse came in to check on me. She said to me, "Your daughter is absolutely adorable; please get your rest." My mind could not rest; as I began to get a warm feeling of love, compassion, I wanted Angelo to be right by my side and knew he was with Graciela while Leila was with Matthew and my nephew Julian.

As much as I wanted the bonding experience with my little girl, I really wanted the help from the nurses to keep an eye on her. She was only brought into my room to be nursed and then returned to the nursery to sleep. I was not understanding my own feelings; I wanted her so much but was afraid I would fail as a parent. So many emotions came over me; it wasn't until a fragile Catholic nun came into my room and prayed for me and with me that I felt light and confident and blessed. I began to feel happy, an overwhelming feeling of joy. That was when the room began to fill up with family and friends through my four days in the hospital. I had my in-laws, my parents, and my friends all come and fellowship and welcome with joy the birth of Graciela Liz. My little Gracie, my little minime.

Matthew was such a little two-year-old helper. He was so adorable and helped me with holding a bottle or getting diapers and wipes out for his little baby sister. Watching over him and looking at how he reacted melted my heart with a tingling feeling of enjoyment. A feeling of happiness, a feeling that I was not alone. I would close my eyes for a quick second and thank God, because without this feeling of not being alone I honestly don't know how I would have been or become the mom I wanted so dearly to be. Everything happens in his timing; I say "his" timing because I was brought up knowing we have a God that oversees all of our troubles, our desires, our helpless feelings, our excitement, our laughter, our cries, our successes, our achievements, our hurts. This God, this being, is always with us every moment of our life's path, our journey.

Two months after Graciela came into this world, my grandfather, whom I loved so dearly, who made me laugh and loved me for me, passed and left this world for the next. I was so heartbroken and distraught that I was not able to go to his funeral in Puerto Rico. I was nursing Graciela and could not leave her, nor did I have the strength to get on the airplane. I had Matthew as well; the trip would have been too much for me just having given birth two months ago by Caesarian section. I felt in my heart he knew I was grieving from where I was. I'd enjoyed the time I spent with him during my pregnancy and the time I'd shared with him with Matthew and my husband. We'd spent time together sitting in my mother's garden in the sunshine, laughing and talking about the good ole times of his upbringing. When he was in Pennsylvania visiting for the summer, he fell ill and did not realize he was having a massive heart attack and needed to have a quadruple-bypass surgery. It was a miracle in itself that I was able to enjoy time with him until right before the birth of Graciela. I will forever remember his scent and of course his sense of humor and jokes. His comfort and his curiosity when putting his hands on my belly to feel Graciela move inside of me. Mi abuelo (my grandfather) Juan Camacho Rodriguez was the hardest-working man I have ever known in this life. He was a man who sacrificed a finger in the early 1930s received a check as an injury and purchase land to raise his siblings on a one hundred acres of coffee land. Abuelo raised all six of his children working the coffee land, and of course I helped out picking coffee on summer school breaks.

I ran my household like a day care: my children had breakfast, morning-circle time, reading and writing time, arts-and-crafts time, outside playtime, and of course naptime. Naptime was the perfect time to prepare dinner and get on the treadmill and get a quick workout or simply sit in meditation. The silent naptime of the children was a time for me to sit in stillness, and I really began to enjoy sitting still; this was a time where I felt something as I prayed. In times like this I felt an energy of appreciation, as if I were being watched from a source that seemed familiar. Familiar is what I began to search for; who and what was it that looked out for me, and why? My journey was to seek this source, and every time I had a chance to sit and think, I felt happy, an inner peace that was hard to share with anyone.

The next two years were dedicated to being the best mommy I could be, focusing on my children's needs. I also fell into the trap of taking care of my husband with his needs, praying for him, making sure that inner self-doubt did not creep up into his life. He had a lot of self-doubt, a dark past of alcoholism and drug abuse that I did not want him to continue to deal with and bring into the lives of my children. With faith and prayer, my husband, Angelo, overcame the statistic that is very prominent in the Puerto Rican community, in which many stay stuck and never get out. So, I thought at this point in my life, I was not praying with faith for my husband. I was praying with FEAR (false evidence appearing real).

My husband struggled with alcohol and self-medication along with his own inner demons, those of self-doubt, insecurities, and childhood emotional and verbal abuse as a teenager. I did not know the problem was deeper than what he was showing me. I started finding his demeanor strange and out of balance. One day he would be aggressively insecure and jealous, and the next he would be so happy, easygoing, and on the move, extremely hyper. I knew the characteristics because I had witnessed my father's behavior after cocaine abuse. I grew up witnessing Mama's family members abuse drugs. I would wake up to the lights of my bedroom on at 1:00 and 2:00 a.m. without Angelo lying in bed. I would find him standing looking out of the window with a strange look on his face. I would ask, "What are you doing?" Angelo would then look at me with a blank stare; I would say, "Go back to bed." At this point I would just stay up and wait until he would go to bed.

This went on for a few months, and when the weekends came along it got worse. I felt like I was his babysitter; it got to the point where I ended up breaking down the bathroom door to find him hunched over the toilet seat with a stench smell of alcohol and unknown pills. This was the breaking point for me and my children. I screamed and cried; Angelo stood up and asked for me to calm down. As he began to say he would not do it again, I did not believe him, and out of anger I packed a few bags for the kids and myself and left the house. I drove to Mama's house and stayed with my parents for a few days. A few days turned into two weeks. I was so angry at Angelo for being weak, for lying to me about self-medicating; I felt duped in this marriage. I knew in my heart my husband needed help, and I did not want other family members to know my situation. Knowing Mama I knew the news of the difficulties I was having in my marriage would get out, and there would be gossip among family. It was something I really was afraid of. My brother Robert called me, asked if I was OK, and wanted to know more details of what was going on. I was not honest with him; I brushed it off by saying, "I'm tired of doing everything around the house and getting no help; I'm exhausted." Robert did go on to say I could always go to his house with the kids to hang out and call him whenever, which I always knew I could; I just did not want him to know what I was really going through at the time, for selfish reasons, due to my own egoistic inner thoughts.

I put Matthew and Graciela to bed, fell to my knees, and prayed to God; I cried with emotions of anger with how my life was going. I needed a change, and I needed my husband. I needed the strong man that I married. I did not want a life that I had witnessed as a child for my children. I wanted out, and I demanded it. As I prayed I got a call from Angelo. He wanted us home; he was sorry. He was going to work on himself and needed my help as well. I felt it in my heart that Angelo was sincere, and I knew I had to be strong for us as a family. I knew God had a plan; I needed to be present. I gathered my things the next morning along with the kids. I went home to work on my family.

A lot of my father's friends and family members had died from a combination of drug and alcohol abuse. I always believed that everything I prayed for with strong faith always came to fruition. I had to be strong and walk in faith and be with my husband. Mama was not happy that I was choosing to be by my husband's side. She wanted me to leave him and stay with her, but I couldn't; I had to do what was right for my children and myself.

Many would question and say, "I have prayed and have gotten nothing out of it." That is because what you actually prayed for was not with your true gut feelings. At the same time, prayer in silence without faith or with the belief that it will never happen is simply a blocking energy of what you truly want. It's important to be bold in what it is you are actually praying for; if it is a change or a desire you must believe in it wholeheartedly. It's speaking it into existence and allowing God, the universe, the angels, to HEAR clearly. HEAR to me is *higher energetic atmospheric reasoning.* You must say your prayer or what it is you truly want in a higher vibration, feel it, say it with deep meaning, and allow the universe, God, to hear it; and it should resonate with your journey at the very present moment. What you ask for and pray for in the present moment will become your past experiences.

Sleepless nights became a norm for me; in order to make sure my husband stayed sober I would be the first one up to care for our children and watch over Angelo. This was something he and I knew we had to deal with together. My parents did not know the details of what was going on; they only knew or perceived that Angelo was just a hard worker. Yes, that was true but he was also being insecure, jealous, and argumentative, which on another note he was and could be at times. The issues were deeper; he had a lot of childhood anger issues, resentment from previous relationships, mistrust, lies, deceit, and verbal abuse that he had endured. I had to be strong for my family. The fight was not easy, but I knew along the way I was not alone: I had my angels' guidance, the love of God over me and within me and through me that was stronger than any challenge coming my way. I was ready for the fight, an invisible fight that I had to hide from the outside world.

During most nights while not being able to sleep, I would get woken up by a source, a shadow, overlooking me, as if this shadow was trying to communicate with me. I would feel a female energy on the side of my bed. I felt calm, but every time the energetic source came in at night, I just knew she was preparing me to grieve. I just knew someone I knew or was familiar with was going to enter the heavens.

CHAPTER 18

Accident, Turning Point, Work-Life Balance

It was a beautiful, bright, sunny Saturday afternoon. I had gotten up early, cleaned the house, and organized as I always did on Saturday mornings. Matthew had a battery-motorized blue minimotorcycle, and Graciela had a little, tiny purple tricycle. After lunchtime I decided to take the kids outside to play, and at the same time I could take in the beautiful fresh air, listen to the wind, and look at the blooming flowers. There were other children outside in the neighborhood as well.

As I was enjoying my children's laughter and smiles, I started to feel off, like an immediate worry of some sort. I all of a sudden remembered that three nights ago I was woken up in the middle of the night by a source. Something shook me as if I needed to be aware of something or know something. I did not know what it was at the moment; I just remember I was afraid and grabbed onto Angelo's arm for comfort and went back to sleep. This feeling while the children were playing outside was very strong. As I was sitting outside enjoying the children playing, we heard a helicopter right over our house; as the children looked with amazement and awe, I saw the lettering reading Penn Hospital, which meant that someone was being airlifted to a hospital in the Philadelphia area. Far to the north of my home, I could hear sirens and an ambulance but did not think anything of it until I received a phone call from Leila. She asked me what I was doing; I told her I was outside with Matthew and Grace, enjoying the outside. I told her the kids were jumping with smiles because they'd just witnessed a helicopter so low over our house. She immediately went on to say the person they were carrying in the helicopter was Edison.

"Edison our cousin?" I responded.

She said, "Yes!"

I said, "No way, what happened?"

She said he was on a motorcycle with no helmet on and fell back and hit his head. At the very moment when Leila was explaining what had happened, I did not think it was as severe as it was, but then again thinking about the helicopter going by us, I realized it must have been extremely severe. I immediately gathered Matthew and Grace and their toys, took them inside, gathered a couple of things and my bag, and drove to Mama's house to check on Isabel and find out what was going on with Edison. As I pulled up to the house, I saw a flood of cars and Titi Isabel; everyone was crying and distraught. Edison was in a medically induced coma; the outcome was not good, as the doctors were deciding to either keep him on life support or let him go. He had severe brain damage, and there was nothing active going on. Mama and Papi had already gone to see him, so I left the children with Mama and went to Philadelphia with Jazmin. I felt the drive to the hospital was the longest ever. All I could think of was whether this was the sign that I had been told would happen, a sign to prepare myself for what could happen. Edison was only twenty-eight years old; he was basically now beginning his life, and he had a young daughter. What made him get on a motorcycle without a helmet on? Whose motorcycle was it? Edison did not have any sisters; Leila and I were like his sisters. We grew up very close; we were all here for each other.

As I walked into his room, his body was connected to many machines—loud, beeping machines—and his skin was cold. I did not understand why he had a large body ice pack on him. As one of the nurses walked in to monitor one of the machines, I asked her why the ice pack was on his body; it was to keep his body levels elevated. I really did not understand, but I felt in my heart that before the machines were turned off, I had to speak to him. I told him I loved him, and I did in my own selfish way ask him why he got on the motorcycle. I asked him if he was in pain, but looking at him lying on the hospital bed, I knew the doctors and nurses made sure he was as comfortable as possible. I did say, we were supposed to see our children grow up, again in my own selfish way. I was sad and angry to see him like that, but as I stood next to him and felt his cold hands, I said, "It's OK. You can go in peace, and one day we will see each other again."

Shortly after that the family was called into a room with the neurologist, who said that Edison had no wavelength in the brain and asked Isabel if she wanted his organs to be donated. Without hesitation she said, "Let him go, and please donate his organs to help others because he would have wanted that as well." Edison crossed over that evening, shortly after the machines were turned off. It was a very sad time for the family and all of his friends. While it was sad, it was as if I could feel his energy as being present. Family and hundreds of friends gathered to view his body and say their goodbyes for now; as he lay in his casket he was dressed just as he would on any ordinary day in a cap, T-shirt, and jeans, with a smile on his face. Isabel was distraught; he was her youngest son who made her laugh and stood by his mother's side whenever she needed him. This was the first time I had ever witnessed a mother lose her son. It broke my heart, knowing the love for a son is unbreakable. It is one of the hardest and saddest situations to face. A piece of your heart is broken and will not be mended until you see your child again on the other side of the veil. All Isabel could do was live her life to the fullest and remember the good memories she shared with her son, my cousin Edison.

This was a turning point in my life. The way my cousin passed over to the other side was no coincidence; it was just meant to be. We all have free will; we never really know when we will take the last breath in this physical world. We must live to the fullest each and every day, and I knew in my heart I wanted to be the best parent to my children, share new things, new experiences with them, teach them what life had to offer and be present by showing them unconditional love in everything that I did for them and for others. I wanted to teach them good morals, respect, family values, hard work, patience, love, and kindness to family and others that they encounter in their journey of life. I wanted to teach them to remember that what we achieve and the materials we gain are all temporary. We do not take the things with us when we depart from this world, but the memories and love continue to live on.

The following year as I prepared Matthew to start kindergarten, I was at a point in my life when I decided it was time to go back to enter the workforce and enter Graciela into day care so that she could begin to prepare for kindergarten and have interactions with other children her age. I found a job in the same area. The universe aligns us in positions to help us along our life's journey. The company I began working for was across the parking lot from the childcare facility; I could actually watch when my son was being picked up and dropped off to and from school.

Advanced Geo Services, an engineering company, was close to my children's school and home; the convenience was perfect. Although I thought I was going to grow with the company and I gained a lot of professional knowledge, I did not feel I belonged there. There was a disconnect with the people who also worked there. The was a lot of masculinity, egoism, biased perception, racial bias, lack of diversity, and lack of professional communication within the company. If you did not make such an amount or have a similar background education, you were not looked at as a human being—such as myself, being of another race. I had befriended the office manager and several other employees, but I came to realize that their friendships were not authentic but rather for gaining my knowledge for their informational purposes.

Once I noticed the company was going to merge with another engineering company that was going down, as I perceived, I noticed they brought all of their employees, and at the same time I began praying to God to remove me from that position. Instead, the universe removed me completely after a few years by what the company did, an internal layoff of employees. As I watched several employees be terminated due to the economic downturn, I noticed I was one of the last ones to be called into office manager's office. I was completely taken aback and did not understand what was going on, as this had never happened to me. As I sat across from my manager and CFO, all I could hear at the present moment was "This had nothing to do with you, as you are a very good employee."

In my own thoughts, negative words came to mind, such as *You bitch, naïve, lying sack of shit*, and as I thought those words, I felt an utter pain in my lower abdomen, then felt empathy because I knew it was hard for her. She was just doing her job. The CFO sat there with complete sadness as I began to cry in disbelief at what I was hearing. There was something over her, a light of being of some sort, and I felt so bad about the negative thoughts. My immediate thoughts as I looked at the CFO were *How am I going to pay for childcare? My children love their school and friends.* I was crying and speaking out loud as to "How am I going to pay my bills, how am I going to provide for my family?" Then

I was told I would continue to get health insurance and a paycheck for a couple of months and then collect unemployment checks until I found another job.

I walked out of the office, gathered my things, hugged everyone I had befriended, and never looked back. I did become bitter and angry at the fact that I felt as though I was better qualified than a couple of employees who were kept as employees, but I also knew God had a plan that would allow me to take this moment and become a better person.

In the following weeks, I continued my daily life as if I were still working, driving the kids to school, coming home, and filing all the necessary paperwork for unemployment. I decided to go back to school and further my education. I worked so hard, taking care of my children, taking care of home and my husband, and also helping my husband acquire a car-service business, as he had already been working for a company for several years and became one of the best in the industry. I thought, *Well, why not go on your own?* This was the beginning of Angelo's journey; I say *his* journey because I helped him succeed in helping us grow as a family without financial worries. It was not my journey; I will go into that later. Nonetheless we did it as a unit together; we pushed forward and kept going. It was everything I had prayed for, walking in faith, staying positive: Angelo became the best husband, father, and best friend anyone could ask for. All I could do daily, every morning, was say, "Thank you, God, for this day." I began to thank everyone I knew who had passed over to the other side because they were also a part of my journey. If I had any type of interaction, I said, "Thank you." I continued to sit in meditation and prayer and began to stay uplifted.

Angelo became really good friends with some of our neighbors; I never really had time to stop and chat with anyone. My main focus was studying and caring for Matthew and Gracie along with their extracurricular activities such as soccer and basketball at the local YMCA. I had a busy schedule. I felt more alive than ever, busier than ever, and this felt really good. It felt great to really spend a lot of quality time. The bitterness and anger dissipated; I really felt good energy around me all the time. While being home a lot and always on the go, I began to feel different when I got around people. I could be standing in line at the grocery store or walking past someone and feel a shift in energy. I would feel either a coldness or a warmth and then see colors around people similar to looking at rainbows, just different flares of light. I never really focused all of the time, as some colors are not my favorite, but whenever I saw bright green or yellow or red, I was drawn to the individual person. I would feel as if something were happening in their life on a personal, deeper level.

I began to have a hard time in public, not because I did not like to be in public but because of the insecurities of Angelo.. He always thought I was deeply looking at others as a form of lust, but it was because I could see what others could not see. It was my own little secret, and sometimes I thought I was weird or crazy or just off. I just knew God had a purpose in me, for me, and through me.

CHAPTER 19

New Job/Career, Chaos in the Workplace, Coworker—Not Friends

I began looking for new employment. Angelo's friend and our neighbor was a magisterial district court judge, and to my astonishment, he offered me a job to work for him. I was left in awe. I did not hesitate and took his offer. I applied online with the local county, and he put the word in for me. I was forever grateful to him. Judge Smith was well loved by the community for his kind, humble, personable characteristics. Many of the officers in the district never really knew how to take his character. I, on the other hand, knew him outside of work and thought he was an awesome individual, always caring and ready to help anyone in need. His longevity in public service spoke for itself as to the type of person he was.

Working for the local county personally I thought was perfect fit for me; the hours worked around my children's school schedule, and I got home early enough to help with homework, dinner, and evening activities. The first few months were great, until the judge announced his retirement. I began to be sad and got to worrying about what would happen next. The office supervisor and I had a good connection; there were four other employees and one part-time person who would come in late mornings.

My career in the district court took off, and I began to learn the processes and procedures really quickly. My first year was very trying with the other women who worked in the office. Every morning walking into the court, I always had a nervous feeling because I never knew what to expect in regards to the demeanor of the ladies. I was the youngest one in the office, and just beginning to know everyone was a task in itself. Judge Smith kept busy in his chambers and only came out when the officers and defendants were ready for him in the courtroom. My supervisor, whom I will call Susana, was a very nice person. At the time I did not realize or understand her frustration. I sometimes took her demeanor to heart at the time and felt horrible going to work some mornings. She would always be short-tempered and aggressive toward the other women. There were Marissa, Yvette, Bridgette, and Anna. Marissa was a very soft-spoken, colorful person. Yvette was the last person I had met; she was on vacation for quite some time when I started. Bridgette was very outspoken and had been working in the court for many years and knew every department. When the moment came to meet Yvette, I was a little taken aback by her demeanor the morning she came into work returning from vacation. She gave me the look of death, like "Where did she come from?" I was almost afraid of looking at her. She was superquiet and a little aggressive. Nonetheless I just knew in my gut working there I would not last. I never knew what kind of day it would turn out to be because everyone would either be superquiet or be very loud with the commotion of the number of traffic hearings there were on any particular day.

I was always such a trusting individual toward others, but what I began to learn was that there was an ugly side to most defendants, and those on the side of the law.. I witnessed racial bias based on the color of someone's skin or based on economic conditions when it came to pleas in the courtroom. I also witnessed attorneys charging different fees based on ethnic background and the injustice from local officers to state police. Judge Smith on most occasions would be for the people; he was very personable and connected with people as I witnessed. He did not judge anyone's background; he could see that some had the ability to turn their lives around, while others needed to be punished accordingly by law for what they did.

As with any job, we all have good and bad days; this particular time in my life was very challenging, and I will never forget how I was poorly treated by other women. Women who were insecure, demanding of others, lonely, jealous, not authentic, close-minded, and simply not happy people, and afraid of change. Working with the public, it's important to be empathetic with the public's needs and separate your personal life from your employment.

While it was very sad seeing Judge Smith retire, we obtained a new judge, a retired police officer from a nearby township. The new judge also brought over a clerk from another nearby district court to be the office supervisor. I was very eager to meet our new supervisor; I thought she was quiet. However, I thought that because of her years of experience, about twenty, she would have known every department and all processes. That was untrue, to say the least; the transition became very difficult in the way that she became comfortable in the position; her demeanor changed and became somewhat negative in the office. The new judge was also kind and quiet, with a small family.

There were a lot of changes that happened over the years and a lot of demands from this supervisor such that going to work became unbearable. The lies, the unauthenticated personality of my supervisor. The disrespect toward other coworkers in the office, and bullying. I was demanded to train new employees when I was not a supervisor.

Having her take credit for work she knew nothing of was very tough. The judge was blind to it, and I can't say he was someone who took leadership and ownership of the district court. It was more ego than leadership qualities, wanting to be in the spotlight but not take on issues that his own supervisor whom he chose could not stand up to.

I prayed daily for a new job or potential transfer to another court. I waited patiently; I was in no rush, as Angelo's business was doing fantastic, and he was gaining new client after new client. Working allowed me to get out of the house and earn my own money and be financially sound. I slowly began to see the positive changes happening in my life due to everything that I had prayed for, walking by faith daily and believing that God had something far greater for me. I ended up graduating at the top 20 percent of class and attaining my degree with honors. I did it while working full time, caring for my children, taking care of the home, and helping my husband with his business. I did it all in the midst of chaos within the workplace. I knew that I was being molded by God and my angel guides, and I also knew that I was protected by the archangel Michael.

CHAPTER 20

Energy Vampires, Near Death

The negative energy in the court over the years took a toll on my body. I ended up being diagnosed with high blood pressure and went into supraventricular tachycardia (SVT) and arrhythmia. I was extremely stressed out and always sick. I soaked in the energy of those around me in the office, and it drained my energy. There are energy vampires everywhere we walk into in our daily life. I had learned to ground myself before walking into my workplace; I would always say, "No weapon formed against me will prosper," and imagine a metal shield around my body as protection. Whenever I felt someone who walked into work with negative energy, I would always ask for protection from the archangel Michael. This was how I was able to cope with negative people in my daily life. Some would think I was crazy, but this helped me stay focused and go along with my daily life, staying in prayer, even if that meant staying positive within my own mental thoughts. You will begin to see positive changes when you simply change your inner thoughts; everything starts to open up for you without trying.

I became very sick while working, and it took several doctor appointments and figuring out what was wrong with me and the debilitating pain I was experiencing. Once it was figured out, I had to have surgery that was life changing and very drastic on the body. At the same time, it was a very emotional type of surgery. I was kept in the hospital overnight and sent home rather quickly. The evening I went home, I was woken up by an unknown source. I felt like I was shaken and saw someone run off. When I came to, no one was in the room; I screamed with pain and felt like I could not take a deep breath. I felt like something was terribly wrong and asked Angelo to call the ambulance. The pain was so bad, all I could do was scream for help, but with each scream I was gasping for air. Once I got to the emergency room, I was taken to radiology and admitted to the hospital as a patient due to internal bleeding. I was observed through the night and felt like I was getting weaker and losing blood. The doctors did not know why I was losing blood, and I was told I needed to go back into surgery and needed to have a blood transfusion. Prior to the second surgery, I really felt as though my body was shutting down; my hands and feet were beginning to get cold, and my blood pressure was dropping. I was going in and out of consciousness, and I remember seeing family who had crossed over. I saw my grandmother, my uncle, and my aunt who passed years and years ago. It was a rather quick meet-and-greet, as if it were not my time.

When I awoke Robert came to visit me on his lunch break, waiting to hear when I would be taken to surgery. We had a long discussion about the afterlife; I explained to him that there is life on the other side.

He did not want to believe it; he said, "No way, that can't be true." He said it in a tone with sadness.

I said, "What is wrong with you?"

He said, "I'm not happy, I just don't want to live anymore. There is no point to life, I'm not happy with my wife and I love my kids. I'm just not happy."

I explained to him, "You have to change your thoughts, get away, go stay with Leila in Florida."

He explained over and over again, "I just don't want to live, life sucks."

I explained that I was not always happy either; we all went through ups and downs. I went on to say, "Life continues when we die, there is no end to it. We begin other jobs and learning processes." I implied that he look for another job, change his environment, and continue to speak to someone because it had helped me years ago. As weak as I was, I needed to use the bathroom. Rob, as gentle as he could be, helped me get out of bed and walked me into the bathroom.

I said a prayer to God as I was being transferred onto the surgical table that if I were to go and not come back to my children, Angelo would take good care of them. My children were the reason I needed to come out of the surgery stronger than ever before. I was so afraid prior to the second surgery; I pleaded with the doctor and the anesthesiologist to be by my side when I awoke. Sure enough both were by my side when I woke up in the recovery room; from what I was told the surgery took hours. I was confused when I saw both by my side because I had actually seen them perform the surgery and discuss their concern of the rush surgery that was performed on me just two days before. I could feel the doctor's concern and unhappiness that he was correcting his coworker's mistake. I could hear the anesthesiologist say, "Poor girl." I was screaming as I looked at my own body, "She needs to be OK!" I could hear a gentle tone of voice of a man say, "Your job is not complete. You are going back to do great things." That was when I opened my eyes in recovery and was so happy to see the doctor. My second surgery went as planned and corrected the issues; I was given the blood transfusion, and the healing process went on. It took some time to heal after having two surgeries in a matter of two days, and I was out of work for almost three months.

However, working in the court system I learned a lot, and I eventually put in a transfer after years working in a square box of an office without windows, and was happy to be free of the tension and micromanagement of both the judge and his supervisor. This came as a shock to both the judge and his supervisor; before I even got to leave that office, the judge's demeanor and energy of the office became thick, and I was able to use some vacation time and leave earlier than expected for the other court. When I got to that court, the judge and the girls who worked in that court came to me and explained that the judge had made a visit to discuss my character. I was shocked and taken aback; I could not believe what I was hearing. Nonetheless, I could not really be surprised, to say the least. I stood firm and proved them wrong and really enjoyed working for a female judge. My life was changing; I was beginning to change and stand up for myself as a person. The new atmosphere was more relaxed and less micromanaged, with effective communication. To say the least, we all got a long exceptionally great. I not only had great coworkers, I built lasting friendships.

CHAPTER 21

Life Challenges, Disconnect

When we begin to have children and work full time, we all get lost in the midst of responsibilities and what life throws at us. We get busy with extracurricular activities, our children's sports, after-school family outings; we forget about taking time out for family time with our immediate family, such as brother, sister, cousin, and in-law relationships.

While I did keep in contact with Leila, Carlos, and Robert, Robert and his wife became distant; his wife always seemed to have Rob on a schedule with her family. Robert always seemed to have to ask his wife to plan a gathering of any kind. For the most part, this was something I understood, having two children of my own with different schedules of their own with sports. We used to schedule amusement-park trips with our children and always enjoy good ole laughter and fun until Mama's oldest sister's daughter (our cousin) moved with her family in close proximity to Robert and his wife's home. She was one cousin of mine whom I never had a close relationship with due to the fact that as a young teenager there was always gossip and hurt toward myself and Leila. That went on for years. Her husband was one of my closest friends growing up; he and I went to high school together. I never had a serious relationship with him other than as friends and neighbors growing up, and I went to the prom with him. I believe she always held some sort of resentment because of that aspect. I could always feel her not-welcome energy, so I began to distance myself from my brother. His demeanor changed over the years; I noticed on birthday occasions that our cousin had her children call my brother Uncle Rob. To my amusement I thought that was always strange. *What is this cousin of ours trying to do?* was one of many thoughts that would come to mind.

She was known to follow her own mother's past karma of having a child and not really knowing who or saying who the father was. I was no one to judge, but this cousin of ours also had alcoholic behavior that my brother began to part take in, and I started to see his character change. He began to be judgmental and distance himself from his own family, the family he grew up with, his blood relatives, his siblings. The happy, go-getting demeanor my brother had was not the same. I knew in my heart that this was not the life or crowd I wanted to surround myself with. As much as I loved my brother, I did not want to be around the drunk Robert. He did not look for his brother or his own sisters but rather hung out with his cousin who I knew had issues with alcohol along with inner issues. All I could do was pray for my brother and his family.

My inner thoughts about my brother went on for a few years. Even though we would always get together on holidays and birthdays, there was always some kind of resentment and feelings of being left out of our brother's life. I know that was true for me and for Leila and Carlos as well. We all felt the distraction of others in our relationship as siblings. In the Puerto Rican culture, family is very important. In most instances when you grow up with a both-parent household, it's about family sticking together. I knew it would all change when Rob married his wife; this was something Mama's sisters always talked about. Robert changed when he got married; he became different.

On November 21, 2016, I received a text from Pito—that is the name I have listed on my phone for my brother Robert. I was shocked, and it began as follows: *Hey Sis, what are you doing?* I replied, *Here cooking dinner.* So I called him; he asked me if I needed any money for Julian. I had told him no, I was fine and did not need any money for him. He told me if I needed money to let him know. I told him I would call him later. But the text continued after I got off the phone with Robert.

He sent a group text in regards to family blasting Leila on Facebook in regards to Grandpa, Mama's father, cosigning a car for her a few years ago. Leila was paying the car note a little late a couple times a month. Mama's youngest sister and another sister both were entertaining the fact that she was falling behind on payments. They blasted her with embarrassment and tortured her with the fact that they were tired of their niece taking advantage of their father.

No one knows what someone is really going through; we need to take a step back and, instead of blasting someone on social media, really get to know the facts. On another note it's neither my business or anyone's business to negatively speak about anyone. We are not here in the physical to post judgment against any one individual, not even oneself. We must respect and treat others with compassion and when someone is in need provide help or guidance in the best way possible.

Robert continued to send texts; he addressed the fact that no one should talk about others, especially if they were family, as it was wrong to do so. Instead of lifting others up, it had been always gossip and drama within the family, and he was tired of it. Mama's youngest sister, Debbie, continued to negatively text discouraging words. I began to think, *This woman is a person of cynicism; she encouraged others in believing that Leila was an awful person on social media.* Robert felt offended and was tired of family blasting our sister. I was getting disheartened and felt demoralized at what I was reading, text after text between my aunt and my brother; it was getting very heated and very uncomfortable. I decided to get off the group text.

CHAPTER 22

Suicide

I went to work the next morning of November 22, 2016; it was a Tuesday. I was so happy we did not have court. I went into the office; as I was drinking my cup of coffee, I felt an urge to call my nephew. However, I looked down at my phone; sure enough it was Julian, my nephew, calling me. I couldn't understand what he was telling me; I said, "Calm down, what's going on?"

He said, "Pito, shot himself in the head, he is DEAD!" Pito was Robert as we knew him.

I screamed so loudly that everyone in the office felt my pain. I immediately fell to the floor in shock and felt a pain along my whole body. I couldn't believe he was dead. I heard the phone drop, and Mama's oldest sister, my aunt, got on the phone and repeated what Julian had just said to me: "Your brother is gone. You should come home and be with your mother."

I had so many questions as to what happened. *How did he get a gun? Where did it come from? I thought all his guns were removed from the house.*

I spoke to him last night! As I got off the phone with my aunt, I immediately called Angelo; we both were in shock. I immediately thought the conversation last night set him off. But it had to be deeper than the texting last night. I couldn't control my emotions, and I felt so bad for the girls in the office.

However, losing a loved one, a sibling, is like losing a part of your own soul, as if it were ripped from your body. It's like all the memories you had as child and adult being torn from every cell of your body. Then, in turn, you begin to think of every negative thought toward everyone and anyone. Grief from a suicide is like no other; there is no preparation, there are no last words, there is no comfort, there is no saying goodbye. There is, in its simplest form, trauma.

The drive to Mama's from work was the longest ever, but thankfully I got there safely. As I walked into the house, I completely lost it and fell to the floor. I could not comprehend why he would leave this world the way he did. The pain of a bullet going through his beautiful head—he was the strongest person I knew. Yes, he confided that he did not want to live this life anymore, but I never thought in a million years he would really go through with ending his life.

As I sat on the kitchen floor, I cried out, "What happened prior to him pulling the trigger of the gun?" I wanted to know. Our cousin who lived close to him went to the house to be with my brother's wife. I was angry about why she would be there, why she had so much to say, why she was even around, why she was trying to make arrangements, why she was simply around. I was angry. I was angry at everyone. My heart ached with pain; the tears that ran down my face, tear after tear until my face was swollen. I thought about the kids; they saw their dad bloodied and lying on the ground for hours until the coroner took his lifeless body. While so many thoughts were running through my mind, I immediately thought of the note he'd sent me titled "My Last Days." He told me if something ever happened to him, I was to read it and always remember it.

From: Robertxxxxx@gmail.com>
Date: MondayxxxxxOctober 2014,-7:33am
Subject: My last days
To: Caceres35xxxx@aol.com>

Life is special. Life is what one makes it to be. Choice in marriage, raising a family. I have 3 beautiful kids I love, adore and hope they become something that will make them prosperous, happy, willing to help others and strong. I'm sure Kxxx will make that happen.

My wife and I once was happy. I don't know how we lost love but it happened this year. Dishonest, the lies, sneakiness but couldn't fool me. You can't trick an old dog new trick because I knew them all. Leaving you I couldn't do. This is the only way I can leave. Not living with a broken heart, not living with worry, not living planning for what's tomorrow. Not being happy sucks. Sorry I was in a dark place and as I was told I can see the light. No one will understand till you reach my point. Sorry to family sorry to my mom, sorry to my sisters, brother and all of my friends. And sorry I didn't ask for help. There are more nosy people out there then they are your friend. Again Sorry.

Sent from my iPhone

Clearly I could understand that he was sorry for what he had done, but this was his only choice according to his own thoughts. But he did not realize that a temporary thought made a drastic, everlasting impact on his children, his wife, his parents and siblings, and so many countless others. I wished I could have been a stronger and better sister to him. He was an ear of encouragement to me; he was always willing to sit and listen to all of my complaints. He was always there for his mother, our mother. I never paid attention to the inner issues he was facing. No one knew that he had quit his job thirty days prior. No one knew that he was having a mental breakdown. His wife knew, and our cousin apparently knew, but what I questioned was why no one spoke up. When I received the note he'd initially left me, I reached out to him and enjoyed his presence for just about two years before he took his life.

The following days after Rob took his life, I started to have synchronistic events that otherwise I never would have paid attention to ever in my life. I started to see blinking lights; I started finding pennies from 1973, which was the year my brother was born. I started to find my cell phone screen with his name on it as if he were calling me or I was going to call him. He was coming to me in my dreams to let me know that, yes, indeed he was sorry for what he did. To ask me to watch over his kids, especially his middle child, my niece, because she was very much like him.

I began to write, pray to God, and sit in meditation; one evening I started to feel a presence over me. Then it was as if I felt nothing but pure awareness, as if I were not myself, just a presence, a soul looking at self. The thoughts and inner voice unknown to me said, *It's OK to grieve, it's OK to have questions. Rob is OK, and his energy will continue to be with everyone, just in another form. Pray for him, do not be sad or angry because one day we will all reunite again. His work here in the physical has ended, but a new beginning has begun. Rob is fine, he is smiling again. He has reunited with family and friends who have gone before us. He has found his spark again. Remember the good happy memories of him; that is what makes him happy.*

One thing I knew for sure was that he loved his wife with every cell in his being. He loved her so much, and because he loved her so much I too had to continue to love her as well. We were all souls having a human life; we all had a life's journey to fulfill. It was none of my business what actually happened between the two in their marriage. I was no one to judge but could offer my guidance and love for my sister-in-law and the children; they shared a part of me.

CHAPTER 23

My Purpose, Spiritual Healer

I want the world to know that while we may all have different backgrounds and situations, good or bad, we are never alone; with just prayer and faith in the divine, all experiences are enlightening but not lasting. Love is forever lasting, and the relationships we build, our character, and how we treat one another can have an everlasting effect on a single person. There are temporary crevices that creep up to make us either strong or disseminate. We have free will; we each have to be guided to the path that feels right in our heart. Going through turmoil is the smaller picture; it's how you react that can change your life.

I know that I'm here to help others heal on a deeper level. Many may ask, "How can you understand?" By looking deep within the soul, I can see that you are more than what you are thinking of; you just have to wake up and see for yourself. It is to be aware of who you really are and what it is you are meant to do in this world. We are not alone in this walk of a journey we call life. We chose the life we live today before we were born; the walk is open, and as we continue it begins to narrow inward. Not one of us on this planet walks alone; many of us may fall prey to loneliness, feeling stuck between a wall and a rock. All we have to do is call upon God the source, our angels and our guides, and those who left the earth for the other side of the veil. We must live life with discernment as we walk in faith and for the good of oneself and others.

The source has always been with me since the day I was born, my true authentic self. The experiences from birth to adult made me the person I am today, strong, courageous, intelligent, sincere, forgiving, compassionate, patient, a winner, walking with spirit and guided by spirit and God source. I'm a better version of me due to my life experiences in the walk of my own journey, and so are you.

Be present; think of what it is you are doing right this moment, because yesterday is no longer, because tomorrow will be the present moment and today will be the past. You are not your angry moments, you are not the discouragement, you are not the ego, you are not the lonely individual, you are not your insecurities, you are not just a mother, father, partner, sister, brother, teenager, grandparent; you are love. Pure love, we are all a part of a larger being of light and love. If you have those thoughts, change them, and you will see the better you comes out. It overcomes the negative, and if you need to cry, cry; it's healing. Play your favorite music, listen to your favorite guru, watch your favorite childhood cartoon. Release the inner childlike laughter. Remove yourself from toxic people, who can be friends, family and those that decrease your energy (energy vampires). Get back to being your authentic self, remember to never allow anyone or anything take your power from you, stand in your power, and do what makes you happy: this is your life that you are living. Love yourself first and foremost. Live for you, and share it with the universe. Live your best life with a smile and keep shining...

Suicide is not a temporary fix to any situation in life. It is a forever-lasting heartache that leaves questions unanswered. There are no what-ifs, "what happened," wishing "I would have known"; there is an immediate judgment, there is immediate blame toward everyone outside of the family and within the family. Suicide is so unexpected to many. I knew deep within that my brother, who was so strong, was hurting deep within, and it was only a matter of time, as he said just two years prior that he wanted to end his life. As much as I spoke to him to counter those thoughts he had, it was only a matter of time before he would do the unthinkable. Put a gun to his beautiful, handsome head and face to end of turmoil of thinking process, his thoughts.

What I want to say to anyone contemplating suicide is that it is a misconception that it will end your life. This is not the case; you have everlasting life whether it is in the physical or spiritual. What I mean by that is your soul continues to live, just in another form. You will never be able to return to your physical body with the family you know. You not only hurt yourself, but you also hurt everyone you have ever known in your life. The guilt you take with you because of the actions you take in this lifetime. There is help; sit in prayer first and call a friend or call a stranger because just a conversation with someone can make a huge difference. You begin to see the world outside of your own that leads to experience, that leads to fellowship, that leads to knowledge, which leads to standing in your own power.

When you sit in mediation or prayer, you begin to feel your vibration rise; you begin to feel the presence of God, the angels, and all your family and friends in spirit. There are no coincidences; there are synchronistic events that are positioned in our lives at the right moments when we focus and have faith in the outcomes that we desire. When you stay positive, you have positive outcomes; when you are angry, sad, lonely, jealous, or insecure, the outcomes are quite different than expected. The journey we call life is all about thriving, having compassion, learning, rising, patience, love, and inner peace. I will always be here to help share the light of God source to wake up the inner amazing strength that we all posses. Continue to see the sun shining, enjoy the green, tall trees, the grass we walk on, the sounds we hear, the hugs we embrace, the foods we share in fellowship; and continue to stay positive with a smile.

ABOUT THE AUTHOR

 Growing up in a small town outside of Philadelphia, Pennsylvania, but born to a Puerto Rican family and cultural background, Lizabeth Caceres always felt different. She was raised in a strict Pentecostal church, and still possesses a very strong faith, which has helped her through many hard times in her life. She works as an advocate for the American Foundation for Suicide Prevention. Helping others heal with grief is one of her greatest passions.

Lizabeth Caceres resides in Pennsylvania with her husband of twenty years and two teenage children, along with a little shitzu. Her hobbies are painting, reading, and spending quality time with her children.

www.ingramcontent.com/pod-product-compliance
Lightning Source LLC
LaVergne TN
LVHW011840060526
838200LV00054B/4112